Literature
and
Theology

More Praise for *Literature and Theology*

"Ralph Wood is a master of both literature and theology. He is thus an erudite guide to literature with deep theological roots and implications. These close readings are not only elegant elucidations of seminal texts in the Christian literary revival; they are also a stimulus to broader reflection on how the 'story-shaped world' of Christian discourse molds the imagination of its faithful-and faith-filled-subcreators."
—Adam Schwartz, Christendom College; Author of *The Third Spring: G. K. Chesterton, Graham Greene, Christopher Dawson & David Jones*

"With his characteristic energy and clarity, Ralph Wood offers compelling readings of seven modern Christian classics, all of which balance faith and imagination with the highest artistry. Their themes and concerns— baptism, vocation, community, martyrdom, hospitality, doubt, and apocalypse—are both ancient and contemporary, and Wood's penetrating insights allow readers to examine familiar works from fresh, new angles."
—Jill Peláez Baumgaertner, Dean of Humanities and Theological Studies, Wheaton College

"*Literature and Theology* is a very fine collection of essays: a perfect primer for anyone interested in exploring the literary representation of theological ideas. Working with some of the greatest modern Christian literature, Ralph Wood offers insightful readings about important issues such as hospitality, vocation, doubt about the goodness of God, and community. Wood's masterful commentary on this religious literature is lively and compelling, drawing the reader more fully into its wisdom."
—Susan Srigley, Associate Professor, Religions and Cultures, Nipissing University, Ontario

"*Literature and Theology* weds intellectual rigor with ecumenical, evangelical vigor. Ralph Wood illuminates the ways in which seven modern stories reflect the narrative heart of Christian faith. In so doing, he discerns the crux, 'the pattern [that] is the action,' in key works of O'Connor, Percy, Tolkien, Eliot, Chesterton, Lewis, and Miller. Wood's deep understanding of Scripture, liturgy, and tradition richly informs his reading of literature. I highly recommend Wood's book-not only to the college professor but also to the common reader who may be seeking aid in understanding these stories as well as a lively, literate way of learning theology."
—Paul J. Contino, Editor of *Christianity and Literature* and Professor of Great Books, Pepperdine University

HORIZONS IN THEOLOGY

Literature and Theology

RALPH C. WOOD

Abingdon Press
Nashville

LITERATURE AND THEOLOGY

Copyright © 2008 by Abingdon Press

This book is printed on acid-free paper.

Library of Congress Cataloging-in-Publication Data

Wood, Ralph C.
Literature and theology / Ralph C. Wood.
  p. cm.
ISBN 978-0-687-49740-9 (binding: adhesive - lay-flat : acid-free paper)
  1. American literature—20th century—History and criticism. 2. Christianity and literature—History—20th century. 3. English literature—20th century—History and criticism. 4. Theology in literature. 5. Fiction—Religious aspects—Christianity. 6. Christian ethics in literature. I. Title.

PS228.C5W66 2008
823'.9109382—dc22

Copyright information continued on page 110.

08 09 10 11 12 13 14 15 16 17—10 9 8 7 6 5 4 3 2 1
MANUFACTURED IN THE UNITED STATES OF AMERICA

Contents

INTRODUCTION

Christianity is a supremely story-centered and story-borne religion. Christians are called to center their lives around the singular Story of God's ordering and reordering of the world. It is not surprising that, as a story-telling people, Christians would have followed the example of their Jewish forebears in being a People of the Book. Though it has many other qualities, the Bible is first and last the narrative of God's people, the recounting of His dealings not only with Jews and Christians but with all the other peoples as well, from the original Creation until the final End. Nor is it any wonder that a people whose lives are sustained by the Grand Drama of God's work in the world should have produced yet more stories and books of their own. This little book of mine is an attempt to relate some of these later stories and books to the One Great Story and Book.

It follows that this is not a theoretical but a practical book. Its aim is to introduce readers to several major texts in the Christian literary tradition, not to explain them exhaustively but rather to invite further exploration of them. In this sense, it is a primer for interpreting those parables and echoes and reflections of the gospel that are to be found in modern novels and poems and plays. Yet it is not an exercise in easy analysis of easy questions. My aim is not to reduce these texts to abstract formulas but rather to enable readers to experience them both imaginatively and theologically. These short interpretations of hugely complex texts are meant to prompt rather than foreclose discussion. I hope indeed that they might assist readers in undergoing something of the same life-reorienting changes that these books have worked on me. As such, it is a confessional book in two senses. It is a display of my chief literary heroes, the men and women whose literary work continues to have a permanent influence on my life. Far from being comforting or consoling, their effect is often disturbing, as we shall discover. It is also a confessional book in being written from an unabashedly Christian viewpoint—namely, according to the premise that the Christian Story is absolutely and definitively true, not only for me and my kind, but potentially for every human being.

From the outset, we must confront the hard truth that the Story here retold is not obvious but scandalous. It is not the story that we would tell ourselves. Such a story would make excuses for our massive crimes and tiny misdemeanors. It would justify our many misdeeds, both great and small. It would exonerate us from all final blame. It would offer solutions, whether simple or complex, that we could ourselves accomplish. Above all, it would not offend by telling us that we are unable to save ourselves. The Christian Story refuses to pursue all of these easier paths. It is indeed an offensive and scandalous Story. It does not report what we *want* to hear, but something far better—what we *ought* to hear and thus, at the deepest level, what we truly long to learn.

Accordingly, we will begin at the beginning—with baptism, the act by which we are initiated into the Christian life. And so we deal first with Flannery O'Connor's disturbing and yet bracing story, "The River." It is a story about baptism, since it is this act, whether it comes early or late, that identifies us publicly as Christians. There we shall see that it is not a gift that we give ourselves; it comes as the church's own sacramental bestowal of the power to live a transformed existence. Because the Christian life is born in baptismal faith—which both requires and enables us to follow the Way of Christ—we shall look next at the question of vocation—the question concerning *why* the Christian life is worth living, especially as it is set alongside other and competing ways of life. Our text for chapter 2 will be Walker Percy's *The Moviegoer*, a novel about one man's attempt to find his vocation while living a massively self-indulgent existence characteristic of our materialistic age.

That the world's ultimate health and hope lie in the justification wrought by Christ's death and resurrection is an ecumenical doctrine shared by virtually all Christians. Thus are Christians meant not to remain passive recipients of Christ's justifying death and resurrection; we are actively summoned into the sanctifying life of obedience and holiness. Yet never is such a life to be pursued in solitude. Christian existence is irreducibly communal. Though it is a book with a pre-Christian setting, J. R. R. Tolkien's *The Lord of the Rings* is perhaps our most persuasive fictional account of the Christian life understood as a venture in companionship. Hence will chapter 3 be devoted to Tolkien's great epic fantasy.

Christian living is an affair of both sorrowful and joyful witness. It often produces a life filled with the peace and the delight that are found in conveying the gospel to those who do not yet believe it or even those who have overtly rejected it. Yet it can also lead believers to the final test of death itself, and thus to martyrdom. In chapter 4, we will examine T. S. Eliot's *Murder in the Cathedral* as a play that dramatically depicts the martyrdom of Thomas Becket, the Archbishop of Canterbury, in the thirteenth century. The other and happier side of Christian witness is nicely embodied in G. K. Chesterton's short and funny novel called *The Ball and the Cross*. Chapter 5 seeks to demonstrate that we Christians make testimony to the unbelieving world not only by our willingness to take the arguments of our opponents seriously, but also by the persuasive and convincing hospitality of our lives.

Christians need to make witness to themselves no less than others, chiefly by admitting that the world's physical pain and spiritual suffering do not make for easy belief. The Psalms contain many more psalms of lament than of praise. The Book of Job contains thirty-nine long chapters of vehement protest against the seeming injustice of God. Thus in chapter 6 will we turn to the problem of doubt about the trustworthiness of God. There we will examine the ultimate and most devastating of all suspicions—that God is monstrously evil rather than supremely good. The text that will be the focus for our wrestling with this severest of all theological questions is C. S. Lewis's *Till We Have Faces*.

Finally, we shall bring things full circle by examining the question of eschatology, the life to come, by way of what are usually called the Four Last Things: death, judgment, heaven, and hell. There in chapter 7 we shall make Walter M. Miller Jr.'s *A Canticle for Leibowitz* our main focus, for it is more than an apocalyptic novel that presages the end of the world. It is, instead, a postapocalyptic work that envisions a world that has *already* been destroyed by nuclear war. It thus poses the crucial question: what would Christians do in the face of such an event, when only a few survivors were left? In answering that question, the novel makes powerful witness to the question that this entire book seeks to answer: How should we Christians be living every day of our lives?

CHAPTER ONE

THE SCANDALOUS BAPTISM OF HARRY ASHFIELD IN FLANNERY O'CONNOR'S "THE RIVER"

Several years ago when I taught Flannery O'Connor's "The River" to an undergraduate class, a student brought me up short by asserting that the parents of Harry Ashfield should have filed charges against Bevel Summers and Mrs. Connin for child abuse. Summers is the river preacher who baptizes young Harry Ashfield, and Mrs. Connin is the Christian woman who brings the boy both to hear and to heed the evangelist's invitation for him to be baptized. Since little Harry drowns himself, in a mistaken attempt to gain yet more of the same significance that he had first found in baptism, the story's real miscreants and malefactors are Summers and Connin—so the student argued, with considerable cogency. Rather than leading the child to new and greater life, the fundamentalist preacher and his fellow believer have practiced the ultimate deceit upon little Harry: they have made him believe that his life's significance lies beyond life. Thus have they engendered the child's needless, indeed his meaningless, death.

In this reading of the story, O'Connor's river preacher and lay evangelist are not well-meant but benighted creatures: they are examples of the Christian treason against the fundamental premise upon which modern existence is built—the notion that physical life itself is the ultimate good, since nothing either precedes or follows it. Such mortalism insists, as Bertrand Russell famously declared, that when we die we rot. With a great cosmic void surrounding us—with literally nothing coming before or following after us—human life has its only justification within its own terms. And since human existence has value in relation to nothing transcending itself, its only worth is found either in the pleasures we can manage to enjoy (in the case of hedonists) or in the good deeds we can manage to accomplish (in the case of moralists). Hence the stark conclusion: Death is the ultimate enemy and remaining alive at all costs is the ultimate good, whether to enjoy more pleasures or else to do more good deeds. To die in devotion to a non-existent kingdom of a non-existent God is thus the ultimate lie.

In "The River" as with all of her stories, O'Connor presses her readers to drastic conclusions. In this regard they share the hard-edged quality of Jesus' parables and sayings. For example, "It is easier for a camel to go through the eye of a needle than for someone who is rich to enter the kingdom of God" (Mark 10:25); or "Sell all that you own and distribute the money to the poor" (Luke 18:22). So must we decide whether Preacher Summers and Mrs. Connin have done Harry a terrible and final violence, or whether they have given him the most important of all gifts—eternal life. There is no humanistic way of avoiding such a drastic either-or. The story's dire outcome cannot be justified by insisting that the child unfortunately literalized the preacher's message and thus mistakenly ended his own life. The story would thus become a trite exercise in the sentimentality that O'Connor despised. She likened sentimentality in both morality and religion to pornography in art: it is a cheap and easy way of achieving a bogus effect. Yet neither does O'Connor encourage any quick and conveniently Christian verdict.

As we have seen, there are good reasons for concluding that Harry Ashfield's baptism is an instance of what Nietzsche called Christian nihilism: a flight from the one and only world into unreality and delusion, into nothingness. "The River" focuses, in fact, on the single act requiring the sharpest moral and religious assessment: the rite of initiation into Christian existence as either the ultimate reality or the ultimate delusion. As the public event that incorporates believers into the visible church, baptism is the sacrament of transferred citizenship from the *civitas terrena* to the *civitas dei*: from the earthly city that is perishing to the City of God that is eternal. If it is not all of these things, then baptism is a snare and a cheat that leads to spiritual and—in this case, quite literally—to physical death.

Flannery O'Connor makes Harry Ashfield's altered allegiance as scandalous and objectionable as possible, so the readers will be compelled to make a dire decision about the boy's baptism and death—whether they are fraudulent and enslaving or truthful and freeing. In fact, the narrator conducts little Harry through all of the essential steps of Christian initiation, but not in the sweet and pretty fashion that turns the baptism of most children into an empty rite of entrance to bourgeois existence. Rather does O'Connor make the boy's entry to eternal life in Christ both violent and uncouth: from a succinct schooling under the unschooled Mrs. Connin, to the proclamation of the divine Word via the boy evangelist Bevel Summers, to an exorcism of a real and present devil, to the monosyllabic confession of faith made by young Harry himself, to his own triune baptism by the river preacher, to a verbal anointing that seals the significance of his immersion, to the confirmation of his baptism in the decision he makes to put himself under the water permanently. Indeed, the boy is offered what might be regarded as his first eucharist, although in horribly negative form: in the seductive candy stick proffered by Mr. Paradise. Thus is Harry Ashfield scandalously or else mistakenly incorporated into the only universal community, the church catholic, the single community comprised of all the baptized. Thus are all readers—whether Catholic or Protestant or Orthodox, whether hedonist or humanist or atheist—faced with their own crisis of decision: whether to regard Harry's thoroughly Christian baptism as a huge mistake or a wondrous gift.

Flannery O'Connor sets the rural and uncultured world of the Connins in stark contrast to the urban and sophisticated life of the Ashfields, the better to lure readers into believing the latter superior to the former. The two-room Connin house is a flimsy structure whose pseudo-brick covering is belied by the family dogs that bed beneath it. The floorboards are so widely spaced that the dogs' tails protrude through the cracks. The walls of the Connin home contain forbidding pictures of elderly relatives, calendars no doubt acquired without cost, and an amateurish depiction of Christ as a carpenter. Though there may be others, we learn of only a single book in the Connin library, a nineteenth-century work entitled "The Life of Jesus Christ for Readers Under Twelve." Mrs. Connin herself is a woman with sparse and lengthy teeth, a skeletal body, a helmet-like hat, and a fundamentalist faith. She is an unattractive reflection of her unattractive environs.

Her family is even less winsome. Mr. Connin has been hospitalized with a cancerous colon after failing to be healed by the ministrations of the Reverend Bevel Summers. He has become an embittered unbeliever. Rather than heeding his wife's injunction to praise God for the life he still has, Mr. Connin refuses all gratitude: "he ain't thanking nobody" (26).* The four Connin children are equally loathsome in

---

*All quotations from "The River" are taken from *A Good Man Is Hard to Find and Other Stories* (New York: Harcourt, Brace, 1977) and are documented by page number within the text.

both their demeanor and their deportment. Sarah Mildred has "her hair up in so many curlers that it glared like the [tin] roof" on the house (27).

Taking advantage of the city kid who has never seen a hog other than Porky Pig in a comic book, the Connin children connive to make sure that naïve little Harry is trampled by the stinking family swine. Thus is the Connin world revealed to be so mean and narrow, so backward and ugly, that it seems to justify Karl Marx's celebrated denunciation of "the idiocy of rural life."

The urbane life of the Ashfields, on the other hand, is characterized by its up-to-date beliefs and habits. Abstract art adorns the Ashfield apartment. When Harry steals the book about Jesus from Mrs. Connin, the Ashfields' sophisticated friends instantly recognize its value as a collector's item. The Ashfields themselves are both party-goers and party-givers. They stay out late and sleep in late, often hungover. Their refrigerator is filled with leftover cocktail snacks, and their tables are littered with over-full ashtrays. They are also philosophical materialists, having taught their son that he is the product of mere natural causes. Harry thus believes that he was made "by a doctor named Sladewall" (31). As a mere accident of nature, the child is a bother and a burden to his parents. They attempt to purchase his love by buying him new toys as soon as he breaks the old ones. When Mrs. Connin comes to collect Harry in the morning, his father gruffly stuffs the boy's arms into his coat. And when Mrs. Ashfield puts him to bed at night, she exhibits little motherly care. Her erotic gait is as reveal-ing as her uncaring kiss: "She hung over him for an instant and brushed her lips against his forehead. Then she got up and moved away, sway-ing her hips lightly through the shaft of light" (42). The world of the Ashfields is marked by mockery above all else. In a house where everything is a joke, Harry himself has learned to treat everything jokingly. Hence his assumption that Bevel Summers is yet another jester, and his mimicry of the evangelist by declaring that he shares the preacher's name.

O'Connor presents her readers with two antithetical worlds, both of them noxious. Yet they are far from equal in value, as the story's action makes clear. The cultured Ashfield world is one-dimensional; it is sealed off in a self-satisfaction that virtually nothing can penetrate. It is not life-giving; it is indeed a burned-out realm, a wasteland, a field of ashes. The Connin world, by contrast, is richly complicated and full of sur-prising promise. Mrs. Connin, for instance, is imbued with a religiosity that fills her with charity, even if her children remain wantonly mean-spirited and her husband bitterly atheistic. Hers is a faith that does not depend on easy and obvious rewards. While the Ashfields live for trivial satisfactions, Mrs. Connin makes heroic sacrifices for her family. She takes care of other folks' children in her own home during the day, after doing cleaning work elsewhere at night. Yet we never hear Mrs. Connin complaining about her hard lot. We learn, on the contrary, that she cares deeply for others, especially young Harry. And when she embraces the boy with the love that he has never known at home, he responds in kind. He clings tightly to the things that he associates with her and her love, even if it means stealing her handkerchief and her book.

Though her regard for young Ashfield is manifestly authentic, Mrs. Connin knows that human love alone will not finally suffice for a boy so bereft as Harry Ashfield. She discerns—perhaps because she does not depend on the world's material benefits—that the child hungers for spiritual satisfaction, that he yearns in some inchoate way for the love of God, that he needs, not generic love or vague philanthropy, therefore, but the quite particular and incarnate love of God. Mrs. Connin thus teaches Harry the most rudimentary of lessons—that he is not the accidental product of an unsponsored and undirected natural process, but that the figure whose portrait Harry hadn't recognized is in fact his creator. "He had been made by a carpenter," she tells him, "named Jesus Christ" (31). She also teaches him that this carpenter is his redeemer, for the picture book shows Jesus salvaging the Gadarene demoniac, driving "a crowd of pigs out of a man" (32). Having learned what horrible creatures pigs can be, Harry is at once fixated on this good news about his ultimate origin, finding that it renders him strangely tranquil: "His mind was dreamy and serene as they walked . . . looking from side to side as if he were entering a strange country" (32).

Mrs. Connin is walking Harry through the woods to a strange country indeed—to the river where Bevel Summers preaches. She knows that Harry needs not merely to be taught the rudiments of the Christian gospel but also to receive the proclaimed Word and to be baptized. Mrs. Connin knows, in sum, that Harry Ashfield needs to be marked with the outward and visible sign of the Faith. He needs to be incorporated into Christ's body called the church. This rustic Protestant's obsession with baptism reveals that Mrs. Connin would likely belong to the Churches of Christ, the American denomination founded in the nineteenth century by Alexander Campbell. One of their central tenets is that baptism is not an empty ritual meant for the socializing of teenagers: it is an act that is utterly essential for salvation, a doctrine that the boy-preacher named Bevel Summers clearly espouses.

O'Connor does not make the eighteen-year-old river preacher a figure easily to be credited, even as she does not make Harry's baptism an event easily to be affirmed. Summers evokes an almost instantly negative response from most of my students. This is yet another shyster evangelist, they say, akin to those whom they have seen on television, always asking for money, if only via the crawl across the bottom of the screen. Bevel Summers has in fact won fame as a preacher who both sings and heals—and who thus would likely have received generous gifts from the beneficiaries of his curative and charismatic gifts. He draws large crowds, as desperate souls gather at the river in the hope that he will perform miracles on the sick and the malformed. Yet on this occasion Summers frustrates their desire. He has come to teach them that there is not one kind of pain but two, even as there are rivers of two different kinds.

There is the terrible physical pain that requires natural and perhaps even supernatural healing. Yet human pain is amenable to human cure. The second kind of pain does not submit to such therapy. This other disease has origins and agonies that are not merely human, and it requires a second kind of river for its healing. Martin Luther referred to this latter pain as the bruised human conscience. It is the essential human illness. It is the pain of sin and guilt and alienation from God and thus also from man. It is the source of all the evils that plague the world—whether the self-abandoning pleasures sought by hedonists or the self-centered injustices fought by humanists. Its cure, therefore, lies in another stream than the clay-draining river that the preacher stands in. When Bevel Summers announces this second cure, he does not speak for himself, therefore, but for the God of the gospel. Though apparently untutored in formal theology, much less in Roman Catholic thought, Summers performs the first act of Christian initiation by purifying the baptismal waters through a proclamation of the true Word.

> "Listen to what I got to say, you people! There ain't but one river and that's the River of Life, made out of Jesus' blood. That's the river you have to lay your pain in, in the River of Faith, in the River of Life, in the River of Love, in the rich red river of Jesus' blood, you people! . . . All the rivers come from that one River and go back to it like it was the ocean sea and if you believe, you can lay your pain in that River and get rid of it because that's the River that was made to carry sin. It's a River full of pain itself, pain itself, moving toward the Kingdom

of Christ, to be washed away, slow, you people, slow as this here old red water river around my feet." (34)

Bevel Summers has a rich analogical imagination because he discerns the essential link between the human and the holy that has been joined in the incarnate Lord whom he proclaims. He likens Jesus' atoning blood to the muddy river that is his liquid pulpit. Nothing would seem to be healed or cleansed by a washing in waters either so muddy or so bloody. Yet Summers perhaps knows William Cowper's eighteenth-century hymn, much beloved by Southern Protestants for its emphasis on the sanguinary character of the atonement: "There Is a Fountain Filled with Blood." The *river* whose healing powers Summers proclaims flows not from any natural source. It is drawn, as Cowper says, "from Emmanuel's veins; /And sinners plunged beneath that flood, / Lose all their guilty stains."

That Bevel Summers' preaching is universally Christian and not provincially fundamentalist is readily evident. Martin Luther and John Calvin both sought to recover what they held to be authentic Catholic teaching—namely, the twin doctrines of *sola gratia* and *sola fide*. Salvation comes solely by grace and solely through faith—each of them enabling the other and neither of them being separable from the other. Thus does the once-accomplished justification by grace alone through Christ's cross issue in a lifelong sanctification of believers through faith alone, as guilty souls are gradually cleansed and redeemed by living in and through the Spirit's abiding presence. Yet the saving result is neither instant nor painless. It often proceeds at the pace of the languid river meandering muddily past Bevel Summers' feet, and it often entails radical self-denials—even death. O'Connor is both catholic and Catholic, therefore, in her insistence that salvation is no instantaneous emotional cure but rather a painful yet joyful conformity—always by means of grace through faith—of sinful human wills to the sinless sacred will. The dread illness of sin, her story reveals, can be healed only as Christians are immersed in the baptismal waters of holy dying and as they are fed, when possible, on the hearing of the Word as well as the eucharistic life of holy living.

Satanic evil being the chief obstacle to such living and dying, it must receive an initial purgation before sinners are baptized. In Roman Catholic baptisms, for example, there is an actual exorcism of the devil. O'Connor famously confessed that, when the devil appears in her work, he is not to be taken as "this or that psychological tendency, but an evil power bent on its own supremacy."[1] O'Connor has this devil show up at Harry's baptism in the person of Mr. Paradise. Having failed to be healed of a cancerous growth that still bulges at his temple, this cynical denier of divine grace is a sort of resentful Miltonian Satan who would rather reign in hell than serve in heaven. That Mr. Paradise is in fact a Luciferian and nihilistic figure is made evident in his manner of fishing: he dangles his line in the water without a hook, convinced that there is nothing to be caught and nothing worth catching. He is also a scoffer, accusing Bevel Summers of having greedy financial motives for his preaching: "Pass the hat and give this kid his money. That's what he's here for" (35). Knowing, on the contrary, that Mr. Paradise has come both to prevent and to destroy faith, Preacher Summers rightly calls for his audience to make a total act of belief—whether in fealty to the demonic or else faith in Christ: "Believe in Jesus or the devil!" he cried. "Testify to one or the other!" (36).

At first Harry Ashfield had found the preacher's name so ludicrous that he mocked it to his face: "My name is Bevvvuuuuul" (37). But he soon discovers that, unlike his parents, Summers is no joker. He is a man who wrestles with realities both holy and demonic, both seen and unseen. When Summers pulls the boy into the water, Mr. Paradise lets out a loud derisory laugh. Harry instantly recognizes this satanic presence and renounces him in a desperate gesture if not by explicit word: he "grasped the back of the preacher's collar and held it tightly" (37). Discerning what is truly evil, the boy is ready to embrace the good. And so Harry makes his clear monosyllabic confession once the preacher has summoned him to eternal life, as the upper case spelling of the operative word indicates:

> "If I Baptize you," the preacher said, "you'll be able to go to the Kingdom of Christ. You'll be washed in the river of suffering, son, and you'll go by the deep river of life. Do you want that?"
> "Yes," the child said, and thought, I won't go to the apartment then, I'll go under the river.
> "You won't be the same again," the preacher said. "You'll count."
> . . . Suddenly the preacher said, "All right, I'm going to Baptize you now," and without more warning, he tightened his hold and swung him upside down and plunged his head into the water. He held him under while he said the words of Baptism and then he jerked him up again and looked sternly at the gasping child. [The child's] eyes were dark and dilated. "You count now," the preacher said. "You didn't even count before." (37–38)

The charge that Connin and Summers have abused naïve little Harry hinges on the preacher's question and the child's positive response to it. How could a mere four-year old possibly comprehend the significance of so momentous a matter? Haven't these two fundamentalist Christians taken cynical and selfish advantage of the impressionable child? The answer lies in discerning what it means to *count*. I contend that the preaching of Bevel Summers is at once so richly suggestive and so starkly simple that the children whom Jesus insisted on being brought to him (Mark 10:14; Luke 8:16) can comprehend it. Even a small child—especially a small child—can detect whether he really matters to his mother and father. Harry has eagerly embraced Mrs. Connin's love because he knows that his parents regard him, like everything else, as a joke. He discerns that, in giving him everything he wants, they have given him nothing. In his own childish way, therefore, Harry desires to have real significance, to be *somebody*, to experience real importance in life. He wants to *count*, not just momentarily but absolutely and permanently.

Young Harry has yet to fathom the implications of his life-altering "Yes," and thus of Summers' sealing claim that he will not remain as he once was, now that he truly "counts." This saving truth becomes evident to him when, back at his city dwelling place, the child is confronted with his parents' mockery of his fledgling faith. His father ridicules the prayers of intercession that Summers had offered for Mrs. Ashfield's "affliction," and she herself—leaning over him with her alcohol-and-cigarette poisoned breath—seems to be unbaptizing him: "She pulled him into a sitting position and he felt as if he had been drawn up from under the river" (41). Though Harry sleeps late the next morning, his parents have not yet risen when he gets up. No doubt remembering the new life that he had encountered the previous day in baptism, the boy passes severe judgment on the wasteland world of his parents: he empties ashtrays onto the floor and rubs their contents into the carpet. But defiant rejection of parental evils will not suffice if young Ashfield is truly to "count." He must also "work out [his] own salvation with fear and trembling" (Phil 2:12), for baptism issues in a transformed life. In a quiet but typically dramatic "moment of grace," as O'Connor called it—a transcendent discernment of the truth and thus a radical turning of the will from self-interest to self-surrender—Harry lies on his back, looking at his damp shoes: "Very slowly, his expression changed as if he were gradually seeing appear what he didn't know he'd been looking for. Then all of a sudden he knew what he wanted to do" (43). With excellent untutored logic, he reasons that he won't have to remain in the deadly lovelessness of his parents' apartment if he plunges himself into the waters wherein, as Summers told him, there is life. And so he strikes out for the river, taking nothing other than "half a package of Life Savers" from his mother's purse. This telling gesture reveals that, in the deadly place Harry is leaving, cheap candy is the nearest equivalent of salvation.

What the Ashfield boy does at the river may appear to be a pathetic act of suicide, a final despairing escape from his parental world. On the contrary, the narrator explicitly declares that Harry seeks lasting life and not quick death: "He intended not to fool with preachers any more but to Baptize himself and to keep on going this time until he found the Kingdom of Christ in the river" (45). Reasoning with the splendid consistency of a four-year-old, he concludes that, because he had been made to count for so much by staying under the water so little, he would count absolutely if he stayed under the water permanently. In theological terms, Harry Ashfield desires not partial but full salvation, not only baptismal grace but also confirming faith. He also knows, at least instinctively, that to be reared by his parents would be to experience a living hell.

Since baptism is an indelible sacrament, it can be performed only once and never by oneself. It's important to note that Harry does not, in fact, baptize himself again. He does not utter the triune baptismal formula at all. Indeed, he almost fails to keep himself under the water, so resistant is the natural buoyancy of his body. The boy himself fears, in fact, that the entire baptismal business may be a deceit, that there may be no radical newness of life, that the world of salvation may be no better than the hellish world of his parents—so near are faith and doubt, so close are salvation and damnation, in O'Connor's world as in life itself.

Young Harry is able to perform his final act of faith only when he sees Mr. Paradise coming after him with a striped candy cane. Here the child performs—albeit in an entirely negative way—the third and culminating act of Christian initiation: the eucharist, the partaking of Christ's own redeeming death through the consecrated bread and wine. In Harry's radically compressed commencement in Christian existence, there is no time for a positive performance of this third act. Yet the child instinctively recognizes and refuses an anti-eucharistic offering when the demonic Mr. Paradise wields it as a phallic candy-stick of sexual seduction. Though humanistic readers may want to see the old man as seeking to save the boy from drowning, O'Connor's symbolism is unmistakable—if only by way of what nearly every schoolchild is taught: Do not accept offers from strangers wanting to give you candy. And so in flight from this Luciferian seducer, Harry finally is able to remain beneath the water. No longer angrily fighting it, he yields graciously to the river's gentle pull: "For an instant he was overcome with surprise; then since he was moving quickly and knew that he was getting somewhere, all his fury and his fear left him" (46).

In the story's final paragraph, we are shown the defeated and frustrated Mr. Paradise bobbing on the surface of the water, as Harry might see him from beneath the river: "Finally, far downstream, the old man rose like some ancient water monster and stood empty-handed, staring with his dull eyes as far down the river line as he could see" (46). So firmly has the boy's baptism brought him into the only undying life that he is able to perform the ultimate *imitatio Christi*, as he finds the kingdom of Christ not in a figurative but a literal death.

The students who insisted that Mrs. Connin and Bevel Summers should be arrested and charged with child abuse were thoroughgoing inhabitants of the late modern age—an age wherein survival has become the ultimate good and death thus the ultimate evil. With such an exaltation of bodily existence as the final good, bodily pain also becomes the final evil, especially when it involves the suffering of children. As O'Connor observed, a sentimental age such as ours makes the suffering of children the supreme criterion for establishing one's moral credentials. Not for a moment does she seek to justify the suffering and death of children. Such horrors are not problems to be scientifically solved, as she said, but mysteries to be faithfully endured.

Yet O'Connor also worried about our almost maniacal dread of pain as well as our even more obsessive concern with the suffering of children. Such seeming goods become abstract and dangerous virtues, she argued, when they are severed from the source of pity and compassion. Their advocates tend, as in the case of my students, to regard suffering and death as the worst of all enemies, and to believe that, if only we could conquer or at least prevent such evils, life then would be supremely happy. Happiness, in turn, is redefined largely as a variety of creature comforts and pleasures. The moral conclusion becomes ludicrous: The purpose of life is to stay alive, indeed never to die. For Christians, by contrast, the chief aim of life is exactly the opposite: The purpose of life is to die rightly and well—namely, in the love and service of God and neighbor by giving up all those things that keep us from such love, by dying to our self-will, by taking up our cross and following Christ. Faith in this crucified Lord is the antidote to our "culture of death," as the late Pope John Paul II called it. Mrs. Connin and Bevel Summers both possess this saving love of God that comes through baptismal faith. Rather than being arrested and prosecuted for child abuse, therefore, they are to be commended for giving little Harry Ashfield the one gift that cannot be taken away: both temporal and eternal salvation. His death thus makes for a supremely happy ending to a supremely happy story.

CHAPTER TWO

THE QUEST FOR CHRISTIAN VOCATION IN WALKER PERCY'S *THE MOVIEGOER*

As the act of initiation into the Christian life, baptism is the origin and not the end of things. And just as baptismal faith is not offered chiefly to the righteous and the good but to the entire human race in its fallenness, so does every human being have a *vocation*. The word derives from the Latin *vocare*—to call. The gospel is no ordinary piece of news but the singular good news, something that "no eye has seen, nor ear heard" (1 Cor 2:9) because it comes from beyond the walls of the world. It is thus a summons, a command, a calling for all people to participate in God's own triune life through God's people called Israel and the New Israel called the church. Jesus' summons makes clear that vocation is a radical life-transforming matter: "[Come,] take up the cross and follow me" (Matt 10:38). "I am the way, and the truth, and the life" (John 14:6). "Repent, and be baptized" (Peter in Acts 2:38). The martyred German theologian Dietrich Bonhoeffer described vocation as living "justified before God." It is thus a lifelong endeavor, as another German theologian, Karl Barth, declared when he called vocation "the process in which a man [or a woman] becomes a Christian."[1] We all have the same vocation, therefore, the vocation shared by every human being, although only a few hear and heed their call. This, of course, is the mystery of divine election and human response: "Many are called, but few are chosen" (Matt 22:14).

Vocation is to be understood as the living of the Christian life: the worship of God and the service of neighbors. There are many public and visible ways of working out our "own salvation with fear and trembling" (Phil 2:12), as Christ's followers fulfill the various earthly duties demanded of them. But while our circumstances may shift and our talents may be applied in differing ways, our vocation remains the same: to

13

love God and neighbor with all our minds and bodies and souls. Another way of putting it is to say that our vocation goes against the grain of our fallen human nature. Hence the hardy resistance offered by many biblical prophets and apostles against their calling, their vocation: Abraham is but a wandering herder of sheep; Moses is a man with a speech impediment who has no talent for leading Israel out of bondage; Jacob wrestles all night with the angel of the Lord and is wounded at the River Jabbok; Jonah whines and sulks because God offers mercy to pagan Nineveh; Jeremiah complains that God deceives and even hides himself; Paul, the greatest of the apostles, is a terrible persecutor of Christians and thus requires an awful blinding on the road to Damascus. In every case, our vocation is, like theirs, to follow the summons of God into the life of salvation, not only for our own sake but chiefly for others. It is usually the case, moreover, that once we have discovered and embraced our vocation, then we also become clear about ordering all our other loves.

I

This is precisely Binx Bolling's problem in Walker Percy's novel entitled *The Moviegoer*. His Aunt Emily Cutrer thinks he should stop wasting his life as a secretary-chasing roué and should, instead, make a positive contribution to society by becoming a medical doctor. She fails to see that Binx is asking a far more fundamental question—not the question of whether he should do *this thing or that*, but whether he should do *anything at all*—the vocational question. He is a twenty-nine-year-old New Orleans stockbroker who has been baptized a Catholic but who, whether due to his own or the church's failing, remains obsessed with what the French philosopher-novelist Albert Camus called the central question for our time: suicide. Given the apparent absence of God, and in view of the unchecked horrors of the twentieth century, why should we not kill ourselves rather than live in a meaningless universe? The echoes of Camus's novel *The Stranger* are to be heard throughout Percy's novel. For Walker Percy no less than Binx Bolling, the question of vocation was acute; Percy's own father and grandfather both committed suicide.

Young Bolling faced this question of vocation already as a child, when his older brother Scott died. His Aunt Emily had told Binx, even then, that all he needed to do was to keep his chin up, not to snuffle, but to maintain an unquivering upper lip, and thus to "act like a soldier." Even then, Binx had silently asked himself, "I could easily act like a soldier. Is that all I had to do?" (4)* The boy could have bucked up and trudged on, but why should he do so without asking the far more pressing questions: Where is Scotty? Does his death mean no more than a dog's? Will he rot like all other animals, never to rise again? These are the questions that Binx Bolling is still asking twenty years later but, alas, getting no better answers from his Aunt Emily:

> "—you have too good a mind to throw away [Aunt Emily continues to lecture Binx]. I don't know what we're doing on this insignificant cinder spinning away in a dark corner of the universe. That is a secret which the high gods have not confided in me. Yet one thing I believe and I believe it with every fibre of my being. A man must live by his lights and do what little he can do as best he can. In this world goodness is destined to be defeated. But a man must go down fighting. That is the victory. To do anything less is to be less than a man."
> She is right. I will say yes. I will say yes even though I do not really know what she is talking about. (54)

Bolling remains vexed by his aunt. She is a sort of stoic humanist who has learned, like many other Americans, to get along without the God of Israel and Christ and the church. For her, as for many of her kind, the church is but a social institution for propping up a dying civilization. She has no need for it. She thinks that she and her noble type can do quite well on their own, finding a bleak victory even in their grim defeat. Binx finds this gospel of self-sufficiency to be empty at its core. If he does finally end by heeding his aunt's call to live a self-sacrificing rather than a self-indulgent life, it will be for utterly different reasons. Bolling hints at those reasons when he complains that the so-called Christians are just as vacuous as anti-Christian moralists such as Aunt Emily:

> As everyone knows, the polls report that 98% of Americans believe in God and the remaining 2% are atheists and agnostics. . . . Am I, in my search, a hundred miles ahead of my fellow Americans or a hundred miles behind them? That is to say: Have 98% of Americans already found what I seek or are they so sunk in everydayness that not even the possibility of a search has occurred to them? (14)

---

*All quotations from Percy are taken from The Moviegoer (New York: Noonday, 1967) and are documented by page number within the text.

By the "search," Binx means something akin to an ultimate quest, a journey with a final destination—in short, what we've been calling a *vocation*. He does not want to live as a man mired in his daily routine as if it could account for life's meaning and value. Such a life would amount, at most, to a few good or ill deeds, perhaps even a few great or horrible ones. Rather than living for nothing more important than himself, Bolling wants to be "onto something," as he says: onto something transcendent, onto something mysterious, onto a reality that exists beyond life while having its presence already here in this life. Yet Binx is so disappointed with all of our culture's substitutes for this "search" that he dedicates himself to living a willfully self-pleasuring life. And so he takes a succession of pretty young secretaries to the Gulf Coast every weekend, there to indulge in the hedonistic life that would soon become rampant in America—what he calls "the sad little happiness of drinks and kisses, a good little car and a warm deep thigh" (136).

Bolling has abandoned his vocational search because all three of the alternatives he has explored seem equally empty. At first he tried reading big books and mastering big ideas, as if an intellectual explanation of the cosmos would satisfy his yearning for a vocation. He soon found, unfortunately, that his "vertical search" led nowhere. The great scientists and philosophers indeed explained the meaning of things, but always within worldly terms that he himself could master. Nowhere did they provide anything like a vocation by making moral and spiritual demands that he could not fulfill on his own.

> During those years [of his *vertical search*] I stood outside the universe and sought to understand it. I lived in my room as an Anyone living Anywhere. . . . The only difficulty was that though the universe was disposed of, I myself was left over. There I lay in my hotel room with my search over yet still obliged to draw one breath and then the next. (69–70)

Percy has in mind the famous quip of the Danish thinker Kierkegaard that the German philosopher Hegel explained everything under the sun except one small thing—what it means to be a human being who, living in the world, must die. Percy also has a character declare, in one of his later novels, that one can make all A's and still flunk ordinary life.

Binx Bolling finds that the cinema also thwarts his search and causes him to fail ordinary living. Little does he know that, by the turn of the twentieth century, the average American college student would have seen nearly a hundred films for every book he or she had read. The problem with the movies, according to Bolling, is that they create an artificial and distanced world that their viewers enter at great cost. Binx is thus a *former* moviegoer who knowingly (rather than naïvely) retains his sense of controlled detachment. Film actors have an aura of exaltation about them, he notes. They seem to dwell on a higher plane than mere mundane life. One of the novel's funniest scenes occurs when a honeymooning couple confronts William Holden on the streets of New Orleans, and the young husband succeeds in keeping his "cool" during his encounter with this ultimately "cool" actor. Yet the suave youth's momentary victory over ordinary existence is fleeting, for he cannot long maintain the feeling of magical reality that the actor evokes.

While the movies often manage to ask ultimate questions, they almost always fall short of ultimate answers. Binx sums up the limits of moviegoing by recounting his response to a film called *Amnesia* starring Ray Milland:

> The movies are onto the search, but they screw it up. The search [as Bolling has thus far experienced it] always ends in despair. They like to show a fellow coming to himself in a strange place—but what does he do? He takes up with the local librarian, sets about proving to the local children what a nice fellow he is, and settles down with a vengeance. In two weeks time he is so sunk in everydayness that he might as well be dead. (13)

"Coming to himself" is one of Walker Percy's most oft-repeated phrases. It describes what happened to the prodigal son in the New Testament, the youth who demanded his inheritance in advance, soon to discover that he had wasted it in a life of self-abandoned sensation, and thus that he desperately needed the mercy of his father. Binx Bolling also hopes "to come to himself" in this biblical sense, to discover a way out of his self-conscious despair.

Even less helpful than great books and the movies are the third alternative: the standard psychological therapies and escapist entertainments and successful careers that numb millions of American souls into living what Thoreau called "lives of quiet desperation." From Eddie and Nell Lovell, a middle-aged couple who have read Kahlil Gibran and examined their values and found them "pretty darned enduring" because books and people are endlessly "fascinating"; to Binx's uncle,

Jules Cutrer, a Catholic who attends church for no discernible reason, since the City of God cannot compete with his unqualified success in the City of Man, where his victory is so complete that his brow is never creased with worry until someone mentions the annual gridiron whipping that L.S.U. administers to his alma mater, Tulane: In every case, Binx is at once amused and appalled by the dead souls surrounding him. Bolling keeps his humor by describing his attitude toward them in proctologic terms—a rumbling in his bowel that heralds a mighty defecation as well as an excretory confession that he has

> inherited no more from my father than a good nose for merde, for every species of shit that flies—my only talent—smelling merde from every quarter, living in fact in the very century of merde, the great shithouse of scientific humanism where needs are satisfied, everyone becomes an anyone, a warm and creative person, and prospers like a dung beetle, and one hundred percent of people are humanists and ninety-eight percent believe in God, and men are dead, dead, dead. . . . (228)

What is a man such as Binx Bolling to do in a world as seemingly alive but actually as dead as middle-class American existence? He develops a double strategy, one tack being negative and the other positive. Binx's cynical and dismissive plan is to live *self-consciously* as nearly everyone else lives *unconsciously*—in a willed and antic despair, in a wickedly satirical mockery of the emptiness of our age. And so he avoids both the fashionable Garden District and the artsy French Quarter by choosing to inhabit a nondescript New Orleans suburb called Gentilly, occupying a basement flat rented from a fireman's widow named Mrs. Schexnaydre. There he mimics and mocks the rampant but unrecognized deadness:

> I am a model tenant and a model citizen and take pleasure in doing all that is expected of me. My wallet is full of identity cards, library cards, credit cards. . . . It is a pleasure to carry out the duties of a citizen and to receive in return a receipt or a neat styrene card with one's name on it certifying, so to speak, one's right to exist. What satisfaction I take in appearing the first day to get my auto tag and brake sticker! I subscribe to *Consumer Reports* and as a consequence I own a first-class television set, an all but silent air conditioner and a very long lasting deodorant. My armpits never stink. (7)

Binx also listens to a nightly radio program called "This I Believe." Contributors call in to declare their faith in such ungrounded values as "freedom, the sacredness of the individual and the brotherhood of man." It's not that these things are intrinsically objectionable but rather that they have been loosed from their metaphysical moorings in both the Greco-Roman and Judeo-Christian traditions. Binx phones in his own hilariously irreverent creed: "Here are the beliefs of John Bickerson Bolling, a moviegoer living in New Orleans . . . I believe in a good kick in the ass. This—I believe" (109).

Yet such swift satirical deliverances to the collective American derrière will not ultimately sustain the vocation-hungry Bolling. Having given up on his vertical search for ultimate meaning in abstractions, Binx embarks more positively on what he calls his "horizontal search." He hopes to find release from his imprisoning self-consciousness by relishing all things particular, concrete, unique—to listen to the rush of grackle wings, to hear the heartbeat of squirrels, to stare at a single kernel of grain long enough (as Martin Luther said) to die of wonder. Binx is searching for something akin to the experience of Dame Julian of Norwich, the medieval English mystic who discerned the entire cosmos contained within a single hazelnut. Such things have no necessity. They simply and mysteriously *are.* And their creation points, however obscurely, to their creator, even if only a human maker: "It gives me a pleasant sense of the goodness of creation to think of the brick and glass and aluminum [at a local Catholic school] being extracted from common dirt. . . . How smooth and well-fitted and thrifty the aluminum feels" (10).

Bolling first discovered his search when, as a soldier, he lay wounded in Korea. Rather than worrying about his injury, he noticed a dung beetle "scratching under the leaves" only six inches from his nose. Where did this insect come from? Why is it here in this time and place? What does it have to do with him, indeed with the whole universe? Is the cosmos itself nothing other than an immeasurably large dung ball? Such questions were prompted by the action of a contemptible bug. It took Binx outside the snail-shell of his own self-absorption into a world of transcendent wonder. He still experiences these moments of awe when he is made aware of the utter mystery of his particularity, the sheer *givenness* of his existence, the astonishment that there is something rather than nothing. The thick density of all things human and natural registers on Binx so profoundly that he dreads travel. Whereas most Americans are delighted by exotic places, he abhors them:

19

It is no small thing for me to make a trip, travel hundreds of miles across the country by night to a strange place and come out where there is a different smell in the air and people have a different way of sticking themselves into the world. . . . Me, it is my fortune and misfortune to know how the spirit-presence of a strange place can enrich a man or rob a man but never leave him alone, how, if a man travels lightly to a hundred strange cities and cares nothing for the risk he takes, he may find himself No one and Nowhere. (98–99)

Binx periodically receives such a summons to become a Somebody dwelling Somewhere on odd and unexpected occasions; for example, on the Wednesday morning of the novel's beginning. He finds himself examining the contents of his pockets lying atop his chest of drawers. He eyes them as if he were a detective looking for clues, asking why he and almost everyone else takes their existence for granted: "A man can look at this little pile on his bureau for thirty years and never once see it. It is as invisible as his own hand" (11).

II

Rather than follow the arduous task of solving this riddle—pursuing the difficult path of his vocation—Binx Bolling has chosen a self-pleasuring life, as we have seen. He mocks nearly everyone and everything for their unconscious despair. Yet he fails to ask whether there may also be something quite ridiculous about himself. Why, for example, does he have no friends outside his next of kin? There are two members of the Bolling family, however, whom Binx cannot ridicule and who thus serve to challenge his neat life of scoffing self-satisfaction. Kate Cutrer is his first cousin by marriage and thus no blood relation. She is the very opposite of the Marcias and Lindas and Sharons whom Binx takes to the beach every weekend until he tires of them and they of him. On the contrary, she is an anxious, thumb-shredding, drug-dependent woman who would seem to hold no attraction for Bolling at all.

Far from being a sex kitten, Kate is a potential suicide who is kept strangely alive by the prospect of killing herself. The liberty of taking her own life proves, at the very least, that she is not a mere anthropoid who, like every other animal, could be made happy by having her needs and drives satisfied. Animals don't slaughter themselves in despair, since physical life is their be-all and end-all. Bolling is drawn to Kate exactly because she is no such well-adjusted creature. She is, instead, a profoundly real woman in her deep need. That they largely fail in their one attempt at sexual intercourse, rather than behaving like two well-trained sexual athletes, endears Kate to Binx. She is the only woman worth marrying because she is terribly real in her suffering. She speaks and acts as one having authority over him, forcing him to face his own scornful deadness of soul. Kate at once damns and summons Bolling by comparing him to Aristotle's impersonal deity: "You are the unmoved mover. You don't need God or anyone else—no credit to you unless it is a credit to be the most self-centered person alive" (197).

Lonnie Smith, Binx's dying and utterly devout Catholic half-brother, is the other figure whom Bolling never derides. This is quite surprising, since Lonnie employs old-fashioned church language of the kind that Bolling usually mocks for being so overused that it no longer registers. Thomas Merton once said, for example, that saying "God is Love" has little more force in our culture than saying "Eat Wheaties." Yet unlike the other Christians whom Binx knows, the wheelchair bound Lonnie uses such religious terms not to express smarmy piety but to engage the living reality of God and his kingdom. Though his death looms near, Lonnie is not panicked. On the contrary, he seeks to make a good death, to offer his "sufferings in reparation for men's indifference to the pierced heart of Jesus Christ" (137). Lonnie teaches Binx that the world's *merde*-smelling apathy and unconcern are signs of something far worse than inward emptiness alone. They mark the absence of something that Bolling himself lacks—namely, a vocation to a Life that lies both within and beyond life. When Lonnie comes to die, Binx has no need either to pity him or to make a final and tearful farewell. On the contrary, as Bolling confesses, "I would not mind . . . trading places with him. His life is a serene business" (137).

Binx's first-person narrative has recorded his thoughts and memories and actions during the week of Mardi Gras. This is altogether appropriate, since Bolling has lived a carnival life, an indulgence of the flesh in the Pauline sense of the word *sarx*—not physical pleasures alone so much as a thoroughly worldly and self-contented existence. Percy seems willing to leave Bolling in a somewhat fuddled state, showing that he has indeed made progress in his search, yet without reaching a clear and certain conclusion: "There is only one thing I can do: listen to people, see how they stick themselves into the world, hand them along a ways in their dark journey and be handed along, and for good and selfish reasons. It only remains to be decided whether such a vocation is best pursued in a service station or—" (233)

Binx breaks off in mid-sentence because Kate interrupts him. Gradually, she has pushed him toward marriage, and he in turn has agreed to leave brokering and womanizing to become a husband and a physician. Both of these acts might be interpreted as Binx's final surrender to his Aunt Emily's demand that he abandon his wastrel ways for a moral and upright existence. Because she gives Binx a terrible reaming out at the end, many readers have assumed that her diatribe expresses Percy's own viewpoint as well as prompting Binx's ethical reform:

> At the great moments of life—success, failure, marriage, death—our kind of folks have always possessed a native instinct for behavior, a natural piety or grace, I don't mind calling it. . . . I will also plead guilty to another charge. The charge is that people belonging to my class think they're better than other people. You're damn right we're better. We're better because we do not shirk our obligations either to ourselves or to others. We do not whine. . . . We do not prize mediocrity for mediocrity's sake. . . . Ours is the only civilization in history which has enshrined mediocrity as its national ideal. Others have been corrupt, but leave it to us to invent the most undistinguished of corruptions. No orgies, no blood running in the street, no babies thrown off cliffs. No, we're sentimental people and we horrify easily. . . . Oh, we are sincere. . . . I don't know anybody nowadays who is not sincere. . . . We are the most sincere Laodiceans who ever got flushed down the sinkhole of history. (222–24)

Emily Cutrer ends her splenetic outburst by asking Binx why none of these things infuriate him as they disgust her. He agrees, of course, that Americans often have mushy minds and hearts, with only lukewarm convictions about things that should matter absolutely. But from the outset we have seen that Bolling finds Emily's call to a proud and heroic defiance of the engulfing mawkishness to be as baseless as the banalities uttered by contributors to "This I Believe." She is a humanist version of their religious vacuity.

It is noteworthy, therefore, that Bolling makes his first step toward Lonnie's kind of life when he sees an African American exiting a New Orleans church on Ash Wednesday. Binx wonders whether this black man is seeking to make his way into the white man's world of business contacts and economic advancement, or whether he has come to repent his sins, to confess that he is made of dust and shall return to it, and thus to embark on the repentant life that leads to resurrection. The man's skin is sufficiently dark to leave Bolling guessing whether he has actually received the imposition of ashes. At last it occurs to Binx that the black man may be an image of himself—one who is trying to remain content in his Mardi Gras life but who is being divinely hounded, despite himself, into both a Lenten and an Easter existence:

> It is impossible to say why he is here. Is it part and parcel of the complex business of coming up in the world? Or is it because he believes that God himself is present here [in this Catholic church] at the corner of Elysian Fields and Bon Enfants? Or is he here for both reasons: through some dim dazzling trick of grace, coming for the one and receiving the other as God's own importunate bonus? (235)

That Bolling declares it "impossible to say" reveals one of Walker Percy's most fundamental convictions. He does not want to confuse art with revelation, and thus to make his novels a vehicle for pseudo-evangelism. Such propagandistic use of fiction would constitute both a religious and an artistic violation. To have had Binx Bolling identify the black man as a true penitent, and then for Binx himself to have knelt before the altar of this Catholic church, in an obvious act of vocational faithfulness, would have led readers to the false notion that their own conversion might be similarly accomplished. Better, in Percy's view, to leave Binx as a permanent ass-kicker, planting "a foot in the right place as the opportunity presents itself" (237).

Yet Percy also lays down hints, for those who have eyes to see and ears to hear, especially in the epilogue that reports on Binx's condition a year later. There we learn that Bolling has indeed embarked on what he calls "my thirtieth year to heaven," echoing Dante's phrase for the journey through hell and purgatory toward paradise. This phrase could still be bitterly ironic if it were not for the event of Lonnie's dying. The soft-hearted Kate feels the need to bid sad farewell to this boy who will not live to see his childhood dreams fulfilled. Binx has no such need, knowing that Lonnie has prepared to go faithfully to his death. Bolling agrees, instead, to remain behind with his several other half-brothers and half-sisters. They ask Lonnie the same question that Binx must have wanted, more than two decades earlier, to ask his Aunt Emily at Scotty's death. "When our Lord raises us up on the last day, will Lonnie still be in a wheelchair or will he be like us?" To Kate's utter incomprehension, Binx answers with the same candor that the children had employed in asking the question: "He'll be like you." Bolling is not seeking to be "sweet" with the children, as Kate thinks. He is speaking the truth that, however little he may yet comprehend it, he knows to be the one thing requisite—that the life of faith and hope and charity that Lonnie lived on earth has been completed and that he dwells forever in God's presence. "Hurray," cry two of the children. "Binx, we love you too." (240). This subtle scene is a deliberate echo of the ending to Fyodor Dostoevsky's *The Brothers Karamazov*. There at the funeral of a child named Ilyusha, Aloysha Karamazov speaks similar words of eschatological hope to a group of boys who had once tormented but who finally learn to love the companion they are burying. *The Moviegoer* itself elicits such a "hurray." Unlike the importunate widow in the New Testament who badgers the judge until he grants her son justice, here it is God who does the beseeching and it is Bolling who is the besought. Against his own stubborn will, Binx has been given his true baptismal life. Having answered this ultimate call, however dimly and still minimally, he can at last pursue his true vocation through marriage and medicine. Though he will certainly remain a sometimes sour and perhaps even a cynical ass-kicker, he will direct his satirical wit also at himself. For the "dim dazzling trick of grace" has been humorously played on Binx Bolling himself. He has begun, if only barely, to be made into what St. Paul calls "a new creation."

CHAPTER THREE

THE CALL TO COMPANIONSHIP IN J. R. R. TOLKIEN'S *THE LORD OF THE RINGS*

The immense popularity of J. R. R. Tolkien's *The Lord of the Rings* has troubled many literary purists who assume that a book with so many millions of readers must offer an easy escape into a fantasy realm of unreality. Exactly the opposite is the case: masses of people young and old have been fascinated with Tolkien's epic novel precisely because it is not an escapist book, but rather because it enables them to confront the most rending of life's problems—the problem of death and destruction, the problem of evil and chaos, the problem of isolation and loneliness. It does so by emphasizing the overwhelming importance of community. None of these problems can be truly confronted, much less solved, in solitude. They must be engaged, instead, by a community devoted to the common good and bound by a common trust. The common good that unites the Nine Walkers is the call to destroy the One Ruling Ring of absolute power, and the common trust is their love for one another as a community knit ever more solidly together. Their Fellowship of the Ring thus forms a far-off echo—yet one resounding ever so clearly—of the company called the body of Christ. From baptism and vocation, therefore, we move naturally to the place where they both lead: to the *sine qua non* of the Christian life—the church.

I

Frodo Baggins, the hobbit-protagonist who stands at the center of this 1200-page work, discovers from the start that there is a fundamental difference between a Quest and an Adventure. Adventures, he learns, are meant for people who are bored or weary and who thus desire something exciting and entertaining. In *The Hobbit*, Bilbo Baggins,

Frodo's uncle, volunteered to join the dwarves when they asked him to help retrieve their stolen treasure from the dragon Smaug. The appropriate subtitle of that earlier book was *There and Back Again*. Though Bilbo was considerably changed by his experiences, his *adventure* left him in rather much the same condition as when he departed; he went out in order to have both dangerous and interesting encounters, and then he came back to the place where he began. A *Quest*, by contrast, is never motivated by a desire to escape either ennui or apathy; it entails no making of oneself available for some quickly-achieved task; and, above all, it produces no return home in a largely unaltered condition. Very much like the Christian life itself, the Tolkienian Quest is marked by a summons to suffering and service that one would not otherwise undertake. Far from volunteering, one called to pilgrimage seeks, if possible, to put it off. Nor does the Quest traverse any neat circle of "there and back again." On the contrary, it leaves the wayfarers so profoundly altered that they can never return home again as they once were. For both good and ill, they are transformed by the Quest—though they are also prepared to enter the life that lies beyond life.

So it is with Frodo Baggins. When he learns that Bilbo has mysteriously acquired the Ring that had been fashioned by the evil creature named Sauron for the domination of the entire inhabited world, he has no desire whatever to be involved with it. Perhaps seeing the addictive grip it has begun to work on Bilbo, Frodo wants nothing to do with the Ring. Hence his poignant protest against the call of the wizard Gandalf to be the Ring-bearer:

> "I am not made for perilous Quests. I wish I had never seen the Ring! Why did it come to me? Why was I chosen?"
> "Such questions cannot be answered," said Gandalf. "You may be sure that it was not for any merit that others do not possess: not for power or wisdom, at any rate. But you have been chosen, and you must therefore use such strength and heart and wits as you have." (60)*

Though the orphaned Frodo is indeed "the best hobbit of the Shire," having been well schooled in the virtues by Bilbo, there is a fundamental mystery about his chosenness. It has a biblical quality in its very oddity.

---

*All quotations from Tolkien are taken from *The Lord of the Rings* (Boston and New York: Houghton Mifflin, 1994) and are documented by page number within the text.

None of the great figures of the faith—Abraham and Sarah, Jacob and Rebekah, Hannah and Samuel, even such kings as Solomon and David, right down to the lowly handmaiden Mary, the fishermen apostles, and their humble rabbi Jesus himself—none of these possesses what the world calls nobility. So it is with Frodo. Like them, he is elected for the Quest in spite of—but, as we shall also learn, *because of*—his being a mere hobbit. This is not to deny, of course, that Frodo could have refused his calling. Yet if he had done so, it is not at all clear that this refusal could have been construed as a genuinely free act, for to reject the freedom that comes with true obedience is to reject freedom itself. To deny the Quest is not to exercise but to surrender freedom. Christian liberty, paradoxical though it remains, is the choice to give up all other choices—and thus to live a life of trusting obedience. Certainly, the denial of his calling would have been Frodo's own deed, for no one compels him to accept his mission. Yet Tolkien as a Christian writer understands that this ultimate summons is a gift like none other. Because it is a radically divine rather than a merely human bestowal of grace, it has the power to enable its very acceptance. Later, at the all-important Council of Elrond, Frodo receives this strange strength to embrace his Quest, as Tolkien's narrator makes evident:

> An overwhelming longing to rest and remain at peace by Bilbo's side in Rivendell filled all his heart. At last with an effort he spoke, and wondered to hear his own words, *as if some other will was using his small voice.* "I will take the Ring," he said, "though I do not know the way" (263–64, emphasis added)

It is important to note that the Quest guarantees Frodo neither a certain path nor a successful outcome. Much of the time he is confused and sometimes he and his fellow travelers are actually lost. He does not know and he often cannot find the way. Well might his mission end in failure, even in disaster. Neither of these outcomes, it must be emphasized, would destroy the validity of his mission. What matters is that Frodo remain faithful to his calling. It is not for him to determine its success. Nor can Frodo undertake to destroy the Ring by his own lonely effort. Just as there is no such thing as a solitary Christian, neither is there any such thing as a solitary Quest: both are profoundly communal undertakings. Though Frodo has no desire to entangle his friends in this terribly uncertain journey, he finds that he cannot embark on his mission without them. His long-time compatriot and Sancho Panza-like side-kick, Samwise Gamgee, insists on accompanying him. So do the two younger hobbits named Merry and Pippin. Together with the full-sized human creatures Boromir and Aragorn, plus the dwarf Gimli and the elf Legolas, as well as the wizard Gandalf—the Nine Walkers form a community of trust and solidarity that is very much akin to what Christians call the church: the body of Christ bonded together in unbreakable oneness of fellowship and sacrifice.

Many aristocratic and pagan cultures have valued friendship. Aristotle declared it to be the excellence that is "most indispensable to life." Yet the ancients esteemed friendship as a quality given chiefly to the strong and the noble and the worthy. Tolkien departs from the classical ideal by making this company into a fellowship of the weak and the needy, the unlike and the unequal. The wizard Gandalf is almost superhuman in his wisdom and power, but the dwarf Gimli is among the most limited of all the free creatures. Yet each has indispensable gifts that make him absolutely indispensable to the Quest. They are bound in utter solidarity, not only in their common promise to destroy the Ruling Ring but also in their abiding *philia*, their loving friendship. Upon discovering that Frodo has tried to leave without taking him and his companion Pippin, the young hobbit Merry puts their case clearly: "You can trust us to stick to you through thick and thin—to the bitter end. And you can trust us to keep any secret of yours—closer than you keep it yourself. But you cannot trust us to let you face trouble alone, and go off without a word. We are your friends, Frodo" (103).

Friendship is a gift of which the evil, those who seek merely their own interest, are incapable. One of the hopes embodied in *The Lord of the Rings* is that the Nine Riders—Sauron's horrible pack of Ringwraiths, the former men who have become disembodied horseback riding ghosts—cannot constitute a company of evil. They are indeed bound together, but only as total slaves to Sauron. They have no freedom and thus no friendship. So, too, the trolls and orcs, the wargs and other malignant creatures whom Sauron has fashioned, always quarrel and fight among themselves, for they care only about their own individual advancement. They are greedy and possessive, never self-surrendering. As the thralls and lackeys of Sauron, they are bent only on mayhem and destruction, never on the construction of anything good. Despite their temporary capacity to collaborate in murder and torture, therefore, Tolkien reminds his readers that there cannot be any lasting Fellowship of the Vile.

It is noteworthy that Tolkien also denies all constructive power to these evil ones. A thoroughgoing follower of St. Augustine, he insists that evil is *privatio boni*: the privation and negation of the good. As such, evil can only twist and corrupt and mock the good: it can never create. Sauron's powers are entirely derivative and parasitic; he is unable to produce anything free and original. Yet in its very negativity, wickedness has a strange allure. Thus does the wise elflord Elrond warn against a preoccupation with evil, lest it be falsely conceived as a power equal to the good and thus worthy of fixed interest: "It is perilous to study too deeply the arts of the Enemy, for good or for ill" (258). Gandalf's fellow wizard Saruman is duped, in fact, by this "fascination of the abomination," as Joseph Conrad called it. Sauron uses one of the silmarils, the magical seeing-stones invented by the elves, to pervert and paralyze the will of Saruman. By showing him the disasters that may eventually befall Middle-earth, Sauron convinces Saruman that he should not resist but rather join the evil lord. Saruman's attempted cooperation with Sauron—seeking to redirect his maleficent means to allegedly good ends—finally and terribly fails, as his accomplice in cruelty, Grima Wormtongue, slits his master's throat. For Tolkien, there can be no true fellowship of the virtuous together with the vicious.

The hideous creature named Gollum reveals the vicious power of evil to distort and ruin everything it touches. Because the Ring gives undying life to its wearer, Gollum has possessed it for five hundred years. But though he has lived longer and longer, he has not lived better and better. As with the power of modern medicine to extend human life ever longer, so does the Ring give Gollum increased longevity but not increased quality of life. Indeed, he is barely recognizable as a hobbit, so shrunken and infantile has he become. Peter Jackson's digitalized Gollum in the film version of *The Lord of the Rings* depicts him with remarkable accuracy: the single strand of hair falling over his bald head makes Gollum appear ancient, while his loincloth might well serve as a child's diaper.

When wearing the Ring, its possessor also becomes magically invisible, disappearing from sight, living as if disembodied, able to accomplish things instantly. For Tolkien, this is the perennial appeal of magic, and he worried that our fascination with so-called labor-saving machines constitutes our own form of magic. The occult arts, whether ancient sorcery or modern machines, seek to overcome the slow processes of time as they work themselves out within both the natural and the human order. It was such shortcuts to excellence that Jesus refused when tempted in the wilderness by the devil, taking instead the slow and arduous path that winds toward Golgotha. Neither will Gandalf abide any effortless substitutes for hard labor. He is not a magician, therefore, but a master craftsman of fire. He has so fully learned the incendiary arts that he weaves himself into his pyrotechnics. So it is with all things worthy of fashioning; they take time and will and patience.

Gollum, by contrast, lacks such willingness to labor and to wait. Though he catches many fish, he is not an accomplished angler. On the contrary, he has used the Ring to make himself invisible while living in caves and fishing in underground streams, catching his prey with his bare hands and consuming it in the raw. It's as if Gollum has repudiated the very basis of civilized life—the cooked meal enjoyed with family and friends. As an almost subhuman creature, Gollum has not a single friend because he shares nothing in common with others. He lives in a dreadful solitude. Because a solitary sufficiency constitutes a less than human life, however, Gollum is starved for companionship. And so he creates a pseudo-community within his own solitariness, always muttering and speaking to himself in the first person plural, while referring to the Ring as "my precious, my precious." Unable to engage others as true persons, Gollum almost always refers to Sam and Frodo as "it."

Yet Gollum is not wholly evil. There is a tiny window-slit of freedom still illumining his darkened heart, reminding him that he was once a hobbit who roamed gladly over grassy fields and flowering meadows, joining with other hobbits in a life of joy and delight. Gandalf in his superior theological wisdom can discern this residual hobbitic goodness remaining in Gollum: Though the threads of his soul are snarled almost beyond any hope of straightening, Gollum remains a creature more to be pitied than despised. One of Tolkien's most fundamental teachings is that evil punishes and finally destroys itself. Yet because it also works dreadful havoc while undergoing its own self-implosion, evil must still—and stoutly—be resisted.

The chief question raised by *The Lord of the Rings* is how rightly to combat the ruinous power of the Ring. When Frodo first learns that Bilbo had the chance to kill the sinister Gollum but declined to do so, he is furious. Not yet having discovered the addictive power of evil, he believes that it should simply be stamped out of existence. And since Gollum had sought to murder Bilbo, Frodo insists that such a killer merits destruction. After all, protests Frodo, Gollum *deserved* death. In his reply to Frodo, Gandalf counsels a radically alternative path, a drastically better way:

"Deserves [death]! I daresay he does. Many that live deserve death. And some that die deserve life. Can you give it to them? Then do not be too eager to deal out death in judgement. For even the very wise cannot see all ends. I have not much hope that Gollum can be cured before he dies, but there is a chance of it. And he is bound up with the fate of the Ring. My heart tells me that he has some part to play yet, for good or ill, before the end; and when that comes *the pity of Bilbo may rule the fate of many*—yours not least." (58, emphasis added)

This becomes the most important speech in the entire book, the italicized words being repeated in all three volumes. It contains the key also to the ending, for without Bilbo's pity toward Gollum, the Ring would not have been destroyed. It also marks the deeply Christian quality of *The Lord of the Rings*. This is not to deny, of course, that Tolkien vigorously avoids all one-to-one allegorical correspondences (for example, equating Gandalf with Christ, or the Ring with the atomic bomb). He also sets his work in a far distant, pre-Christian age—long before the calling of Abraham and the coming of Christ. Even so, Tolkien silently imbues his novel with profound Christian concerns and convictions.

Pity, for example, is generally regarded as a vice in the non-Christian world. Only the weak and the hapless victims of chance—the pathetic ones who cannot manage their own lives—are to be pitied. To have mercy on such egregious evildoers as Saruman and Gollum would be considered an act of rank injustice, for it means that they would not be given their due. Gandalf's refusal of such noble pagan wisdom lies at the heart of his acute moral and spiritual insight. Few of us would live long if granted absolute justice, he observes, since everyone is guilty of deeds that, at least in their cumulative effect, deserve death. And some who do not merit such punishment nonetheless die innocently. Gandalf discerns, therefore, that mercy is a greater good than justice. For it grants such a malefactor as Gollum the chance for redemption—the opportunity neither to condone nor forget the ills he has committed, but rather to overcome them in a life of repented evil and restored justice. The aim of communal life is to transform the receiver of mercy into the giver of mercy.

Frodo reluctantly grants Gollum such forgiveness. He refuses, for example, to keep Gollum tethered lest he flee. Frodo sees that such a chaining of Gollum would be profoundly demeaning, denying him what little of his hobbitic humanity is left. Though his motives are always self-serving, Gollum nevertheless leads Frodo and Sam out of trouble again and again, until finally they arrive at the Cracks of Mount Doom, the volcanic fires that alone are hot enough to dissolve the Ruling Ring. Without these sustained acts of trust in Gollum, the Quest would have failed. Yet Sam always remains suspicious of Gollum, always assuming the worst, calling him "Slinker" and "Stinker" and "Sneak," thus denying (at least implicitly) that the shriveled creature is capable of redemption. Sam is largely justified in his distrust of Gollum, for he has possessed the Ring for so long that it has gained virtually complete control over him. Yet Tolkien repeatedly depicts Gollum as caught in a fierce internal debate about whether he should keep his promise not to touch the Ring, or else to break his oath by seizing the dread loop of coercive power that hangs from Frodo's neck. Repeatedly, the good in Gollum triumphs over his malice and greed, but just barely. Gollum thus seems to be slowly creeping back into the possibility of restored life and friendship with Frodo and Sam.

Perhaps the most poignant scene in the entire book—the one Tolkien acknowledged to be the most saddening for him to compose— is the one occasion when Gollum finds Sam asleep rather than awake and keeping guard by Frodo's side. If ever there were apt occasion for Gollum to steal the Ring, this surely is it. Instead, he reaches tenderly for Frodo's knee, in an almost caressing touch. It seems clear that he wants, at last, to be restored to communion with his fellow hobbits, and thus to leave behind his life of conniving distrust. But Frodo stirs in his sleep—perhaps in a nightmare vision of the task before him—at the very moment Gollum touches his knee. When Frodo cries out in his dream, Sam is awakened and begins immediately to accuse Gollum of evil intentions. Rather than plead his innocence, Gollum retreats into his old resentful self, never more to emerge from it. "Almost spider-like he looked now, crouched back on his bent limbs, with his protruding eyes. The fleeting moment had passed, beyond recall" (699). Having always expected Gollum to do evil, Sam gives the wretched hobbit a final excuse to fulfill such sinister misgivings. When evil is returned for evil, Tolkien suggests, the result is evil compounded. Not until Sam himself experiences the addictive power of the Ring will he sympathize with Gollum.

Christians are commanded never to return evil for evil but always good instead. Yet since Sauron knows and does only evil things, good can make no appeal to him. Tolkien reveals a third alternative, therefore, when facing a malignancy that is absolute—namely, to forswear all attempts to use evil for the sake of good. As we have seen, Saruman wanted to join forces with Sauron and thus to employ the Ring's ruthless might for such peaceable purposes as Knowledge, Rule, and Order. This substitution of means for ends is, for Tolkien, the essence of evil. Boromir, by contrast, wants to use the Ring to defeat Sauron. As a brave and fearless warrior, he is not afraid to die. What Boromir fails to understand is that his one ruling virtue, courage, cannot stand alone and apart from the other virtues. Since he lacks prudence and justice and temperance—the remaining classical virtues—Boromir's very strength would undo him. Once he defeated the Dark Lord, Boromir would himself become a new and even more malevolent version of Sauron.

Oblivious to such truth, Boromir attempts to seize the Ring from Frodo—though he immediately sees the folly of his deed and repents of it. He also dies a redemptive death while slaying many orcs. Aragorn's final blessing and forgiveness of Boromir is one of the book's most moving scenes, as it demonstrates yet again the power of forgiveness. Even so, it remains sadly noteworthy that the Fellowship of the Ring is broken, not by an enemy Ringwraith, but by one of its own members: the man Boromir. The community of the good is thus corrupted from within by the unfaithful even more than from without by the hostile.

Just as Boromir foolishly sought the Ring, Gandalf and Galadriel wisely refuse it. They have the wisdom that Boromir and Saruman lack, for they know that their strengths would be magnified into idolatrous proportions if they possessed such absolute power. Gandalf's great mercy would be fatal, as he would use the Ring to grant pardon to everyone for everything, without regard to their repentance and reform. Galadriel's beauty would be exalted to such heights that it would become mesmerizing. Rather than admiring her loveliness freely, others would slavishly fall down before her in sheer adoration. Thus would a Dark Queen named Galadriel replace the Dark Lord named Sauron.

The key to the eventual success of the Quest is revealed early in the epic, at the Council of Elrond, when Gandalf makes the staggering suggestion that the Company wreck Sauron's scheme to recapture the Ring by destroying it rather than employing it for their own supposedly benign uses. Gandalf shrewdly discerns that the wicked always expect wickedness from others. Sauron assumes that, having acquired the Ring of total power, the Company will want to increase that power until, like him, they can dominate the world. This is indeed the logic of greed and pride: The rich want more riches, the powerful greater power, and the famous still larger fame. The only hope for the Nine Walkers is the same paradoxical hope that sustains Christians: the folly of the cross, the holy foolishness, not of seeking, but rather of surrendering all desire for domination. Hence Gandalf's revolutionary call:

> It is wisdom to recognize necessity, when all other courses have been weighed, though as folly it may appear to those who cling to false hope. Well, let folly be our cloak, a veil before the eyes of the Enemy! For he is very wise, and weighs all things to a nicety in the scales of his malice. But the only measure that he knows is desire, desire for power; and so he judges all hearts. Into his heart the thought will not enter that any will refuse it [such power], that having the Ring we may seek to destroy it. If we seek this, we shall put him out of reckoning. (262)

There is neither time nor space to follow the many serendipities and calamities that the Fellowship encounters. Suffice it to say that, even though the Company is eventually fragmented, no one ever travels entirely alone. They form little subcommunities of two or three, for their terrible trek could never have been completed if they had worked as mere individuals rather than as a company. They repeatedly reveal themselves, moreover, to be a community of utter self-sacrifice, willing to be led like sheep to Sauron's slaughter in order for Frodo and Sam to make their way to the Cracks of Mount Doom. It is not the Company's survival that counts but rather their faithfulness to the Quest. Surprising allies also come to their aid, especially the Riders of Rohan with their valiant King Théoden, as well as the Sleeping Dead whom Aragorn arouses. He leads them to atone for their earlier promise breaking by defeating the Corsairs of Umbar, thus breaking the pirates' siege of Minas Tirith.

Not least of these ancillary forces are the noble warrior Faramir and his eventual bride Éowyn. Faramir is Tolkien's figure of the true Christian soldier, one who despises killing and will go to war only under the most drastic provocations. Éowyn is the lionhearted woman who disguises herself as a man in order to slay Angmar, king of the Ringwraiths. But while she entered battle in order to gain the fame that she had been wrongly denied as a woman, Éowyn gradually learns the lesson that Aragorn had sought earlier to teach her: "A time may come soon when none will return [from battle]. Then there will be need of valour without renown, for none shall remember the deeds that are done in the last defence of your homes. Yet the deeds will not be less valiant because they are unpraised" (767). In a darkening world such as ours, Tolkien the Christian thus makes evident the intrinsic nature of good: it requires neither victory nor validating reward. Neither does Tolkien shrink from confronting the ultimate power of evil to overwhelm human resistance. In fact, Frodo's failure at the Cracks of Doom is the most surprising and telling moment of the whole novel. The nearer his approach to the volcanic mountain where the Ring was originally forged by Sauron, the more it drains him of both physical and moral strength. He seems forlorn, defeated, doomed to failure: "I am naked in the dark, Sam, and there is no veil between me and the wheel of fire [i.e., the Ring]. I begin to see it even with my waking eyes, and all else fades" (916). Frodo is made so weary by his trials that he can no longer walk but must be carried up the dread mountain by his dear friend Sam. Yet to the reader's utter astonishment, Frodo musters one final act of defiance against the Ring, as he approaches the volcanic fissure. Flicking away the attacking Gollum as if he were an insect, Frodo brings himself to his greatest moment of faithful freedom by seeking to destroy the Ring. Yet his noblest act is quickly twisted into his most ignominious failure, as he finally refuses to surrender the Ring: . . . "I do not choose now to do what I came to do. I will not do this deed. The Ring is mine!" (924).

This scene has rightly troubled readers. Why would Tolkien bring his protagonist on such a long and arduous journey, only to have him fail at the final and crucial point? The answer lies in the quality of Frodo's voice as he speaks the fearful words of defiance. It is clearly not his own voice nor even Sauron's voice that comes from Frodo's mouth but rather the voice of the Ring itself. His freedom of will has been completely overwhelmed by the coercive power of evil. Indeed, Frodo is made virtually into the Ring's puppet, as the demonic force ventriloquizes its own words through the hobbit's speech. Such, Tolkien suggests, is the nature of cosmic evil. In the language of St. Paul, we struggle not against flesh and blood but against the principalities and powers of the air.

Such a final and dispiriting defeat would seem to bring Tolkien's epic work to an almost unbearably sad end, thus portending nothing but ill for such communities as the Fellowship of the Ring and its counterpart in the Christian churches. Yet from the beginning Tolkien has laid down hints that there is more than a single power at work in these dire events; another greater, even providential power is also moving behind the scenes. What appeared to be chance and luck was also, at another level, a matter of divine design. Bilbo didn't just "happen" to find the Ring; he was *meant* to do so. Neither are Frodo's repeated acts of forgiveness toward Gollum to be construed as mere hobbitic kindness. Such deeds of mercy are clearly enabled by a power greater than Frodo's own good will. It is these persistent demonstrations of pity that keep Gollum alive and thus bring him to complete the Quest, albeit unintentionally, that the Company itself could not positively accomplish. No sooner has Frodo put on the Ring, in fact, than Gollum bites off the finger that wears it. Thinking himself at last victorious, and thus dancing a triumphant jig of joy, Gollum tumbles backward into the all-melting volcanic lava, destroying himself and the Ring. The Quest is thus finally accomplished not only through the faithfulness of the Company but also through the subtle, merciful, and providential ordering of a seemingly chaotic world.

II

This, then, is the hope that J. R. R. Tolkien holds out for the Company of the Faithful, whether in the church or in a work of fantasy such as *The Lord of the Rings*. The most important of all victories—the refusal of all domination and coercion by the self-surrendering community of the faithful—can be won by the humble and the unpretentious as not by the proud and boastful. These latter types are prone to self-aggrandizement, always seeking greater power and possessions. The life of faith can be accomplished only by the fellowship of the weak who know that what the world counts as weakness is their strange strength. It's not a calling, as we have seen, that anyone volunteers to undertake. The Quest is a summons that comes to the least likely and the least able and even the least willing, precisely because they alone possess a power unknown to the evil ones: the power that refuses power over the wills and bodies of others. Elrond gives voice to this calling and this Quest early in the novel as he sends the Company on their way:

> "The road must be trod, but it will be very hard. And neither strength nor wisdom [as the world construes them] will carry us far upon it. . . . Yet such is oft the course of deeds that move the wheels of the world: small hands do them because they must, while the eyes of the great are elsewhere" (262).

CHAPTER FOUR

THE WITNESS MADE BY MARTYRDOM IN T. S. ELIOT'S *MURDER IN THE CATHEDRAL*

The blood of the martyrs is the seed of the church." So wrote Tertullian in the third century. The great pagan virtue of fortitude or courage was realized most fully in warfare through the slaying of enemies. Early in our tradition, Christians began radically to revise, even to reverse and transform, the virtue of courage into the virtue of martyrdom. The granting of hospitality to strangers and even enemies is already a biblical mandate in the Old Testament, and we have seen how this is the overarching theme and driving motive of *The Lord of the Rings*. The New Testament clearly makes the forgiveness of foes its central theme. It lies, in fact, at the heart of our Lord's model prayer: "forgive us our trespasses as we forgive those who have trespassed against us." So do the repeated New Testament injunctions for Christians *not* to return evil for evil serve drastically to challenge the notion that Christians should be eager to put enemies to death. Since we were ourselves the former enemies of God, how can Christians not extend mercy to our own antagonists? Stephen and Peter and Paul are among the New Testament martyrs, though many more would follow.

Because this is no simple matter, and because not to resist enemies is sometimes to sanction the slaughter of innocents, the church worked out its *just war* teachings, a carefully specified set of conditions under which Christians are willing to wage war. Even so, a life of suffering for Christ rather than vengeance against adversaries remains the most telling witness for the faith:

> For to this you have been called, because Christ also suffered for you, leaving you an example, so that you should follow in his steps. "He committed no sin, and no deceit was found in his mouth." When he

was abused, he did not return abuse; when he suffered, he did not threaten; but he entrusted himself to the one who judges justly. He himself bore our sins in his body on the cross, so that, free from sins, we might live for righteousness; by his wounds you have been healed. (1 Pet 2:21-24)

There is a deep correlation between knowing and doing, between what we know and what our knowledge prompts us to do. Christians came to believe, therefore, that the deepest love is the love of enemies, those who attack us and our friends. The highest form of suffering, in turn, is the willingness to be killed rather than to kill for the sake of the gospel. In fact, it is almost impossible to imagine the spread of the gospel without the witness of the martyrs—so much so, in fact, that the New Testament word *martus* was eventually translated not only as "witness" but also "martyr," just as the related Greek term *mystérion* was rendered not only as "mystery" but also "sacrament."

It is a mistake to assume that it was only the early church that suffered mass martyrdoms under pagan persecution. There were more Christian martyrs in the twentieth century, in fact, than in all previous centuries combined, just as there were more people killed by violent means in that same century than in all preceding centuries: roughly one hundred 80 million souls slaughtered, most of them by their own governments, approximately 45.5 million of them being Christian martyrs. To encounter such martyrdoms in an instructive way, we would do well directly to engage such witnesses as Maximilian Kolbe, Paul Schneider, and Edith Stein by reading their remarkable stories, especially Dietrich Bonhoeffer's *Letters and Papers from Prison*. Even then, we would still need a theological interpreter to determine the quality of such martyrdoms. Artists possess such interpretive power. They depict the images and scenes, the action and the dialogue, that reveal the meaning and significance of human words and deeds. They do not objectively hold up a mirror to life, nor do they subjectively create reality out of their own inner resources. Rather, they order life's "blooming, buzzing confusion," as William James famously called it, by fitting matter that is often chaotic to the artistic form that it requires, seeing it whole and thus revealing its truth.

Robert Bolt's *A Man for All Seasons* is such a dramatic and artistic account of Sir/Saint Thomas More's martyrdom at the hands of his old friend, King Henry VIII, who had made him Lord Chancellor of all England. Because More was unwilling to sanction Henry's assertion of his own political authority over Christ and his church, the king had him beheaded. Visiting him in prison, More's wife Alice pleads that he relent in his deadly opposition to Henry, that he not thus "elect yourself a hero." More responds by reminding her of the perennial Christian call to an unelected heroism, leading even unto martyrdom:

> "If we lived in a State where virtue was profitable, common sense would make us good, and greed would make us saintly. And we'd live like animals or angels in the happy land that needs no heroes. But since in fact we see that avarice, anger, pride, sloth, lust and stupidity commonly profit beyond humility, chastity, fortitude, justice and thought, and [we] have to choose, to be human at all . . . why then perhaps we *must* stand fast a little—even at the risk of being heroes."[1]

Murder in the Cathedral is T. S. Eliot's similarly sympathetic portrait of Thomas Becket, the twelfth-century archbishop of Canterbury who, like Thomas More, also served as the Chancellor of England. He was martyred at the hands of Henry II over another issue concerning the relation of the church to the crown. It's as if both playwrights discerned that the chief quandary for the church of our time would be its relation to secular totalitarianism as it was anticipated by the religious and state authoritarianism of the twelfth and sixteenth centuries.

The deadly division between Becket and Henry concerned the king's insistence that the state had the right to punish lawbreaking clergy beyond the church's own chastisement of them. Our modern sympathies are likely to lie with King Henry, especially since pastors and priests often commit crimes that the churches either excuse or cover up. Yet we would do well, before too eagerly measuring an earlier age by the standards of our own, to consider G. K. Chesterton's assessment of Becket's role in relation to medieval Catholicism:

> [T]he first fact about the Church was that it created a machinery of pardon, where the State could only work a machinery of punishment. It claimed to be a divine detective who helped the criminal to escape by a plea of guilty. It was, therefore, in the very nature of the institution, that when it did punish materially it punished more lightly. . . . Our world, then, cannot understand St. Thomas [of Canterbury] . . . without accepting a flaming and even fantastic charity, by which the great Archbishop undoubtedly stands for the victims of this world, where the wheel of fortune grinds the faces of the poor.[2]

Eliot's *Murder in the Cathedral* offers an especially powerful understanding of martyrdom as the final form of Christian witness, precisely because it makes no easy exoneration of Thomas. On the contrary, it probes the paradox that even this highest kind of Christian testimony can be sinfully corrupted by self-interest. In so doing, Eliot demonstrates why a right understanding of Christian action is as much needed in our time as in earlier times.

I

Eliot gives the Chorus an uncommonly large role in the play, recalling its similarly central place in Greek tragedy. The Chorus voices both the valid and the selfish concerns of the people, those who are most likely to gain or lose from Becket's death. Thomas is returning from a seven-year absence in France, and these poor women of Canterbury are fearful that his reappearance will provoke Henry to a punitive reaction, thus endangering their precarious peace. They represent the temptation to maintain the status quo, to stand aside from hard decisions, and to be content with life's ordinary round, the dull and endless cycle of what they call "living and partly living":

> O Thomas our Lord, leave us and leave us be, in our humble and tarnished frame of existence, leave us; do not ask us
> To stand to the doom on the house, the doom on the Archbishop, the doom on the world.
> Archbishop, secure and assured of your fate, unaffrayed among the shades, do you realise what you ask, do you realise what it means
> To the small folk drawn into the pattern of fate, the small folk who live among small things,
> The strain on the brain of the small folk who stand to the doom of the house, the doom of their lord, the doom of the world? (20–21) *

Eliot employs two older words here in order to reveal the depth of the Chorus's terror. *Unaffrayed* means more than merely "unfearful"; it signifies that Thomas is "unstartled" and "undisturbed"—so serene is his confidence that, even if he is murdered, he will be recognized as a martyr and thus beatified as saint. The workaday Christians who make up

---

*All quotations from Eliot are taken from *Murder in the Cathedral* (New York: Harcourt, Brace & World, 1963) and are documented by page number within the text.

the Chorus lack such assurance; on the contrary, if they are sucked into the dreadful vortex of the archbishop's assassination, their lives will end not only in terror but also in seeming insignificance. These sincere souls lack any way of distinguishing between the earthly motions of fate and the divine motions of eternity. And so they remain terrified of their approaching *doom*—a word whose meaning here indicates "judgment" more than "defeat." Their world is about to be judged and found horribly empty of divinity. For these simple Christian souls, Thomas Becket is the lynchpin that holds the wheel of the universe in place. Without him (and without the church whose hierarchical and communal order he signifies) they feel themselves lost within a "void apart. . . . in a final fear which none understands" (20).

What makes *Murder in the Cathedral* such a convincing portrayal of martyrdom is that the archbishop himself is made to feel the same terror that shatters the Chorus. He is faced with four tempters who offer him alternative ways of avoiding martyrdom, just as Satan similarly sought to turn Jesus away from the path toward Golgotha. The First Tempter lures Becket back to the epicurean pleasures of his youthful *past*—a life of feasting and dancing, a celebration of the sensuous delights. Instead of promising him the power to turn stones into bread, this demonic voice poetically tempts Thomas to the carefree life of the court:

> Fluting in the meadows, viols in the hall,
> Laughter and apple-blossom floating on the water,
> Singing at nightfall, whispering in chambers,
> Fires devouring the winter season,
> Eating up the darkness, with wit and wine and wisdom!
> Now that the King and you are in amity,
> Clergy and laity may return to gaiety,
> Mirth and sportfulness need not walk warily. (24)

Knowing that the insouciance of his youth is finished and thus that its delights are impossible to restore, the archbishop remains largely unmoved by this appeal to adolescent pleasures. The Second Tempter offers a far more magnetic allurement—for Thomas to employ his religious power for the sake of *present* accomplishment. Through a political alliance with King Henry, Becket could massively improve the might of the English state. Such combined effort might be as miraculous as Satan's temptation to leap from the temple wall and to be rescued by

41

angels. Yet in Thomas (as not in Jesus) we begin to detect a note of overconfidence, as if he were utterly incorruptible, as if the gospel had nothing to do with mundane affairs, as if all attempts to work the kingdom's coming on earth were mistaken, serving only to worsen things:

> Temporal power, to build a good world,
> To keep order, as the world knows order.
> Those who put their faith in worldly order
> Not controlled by the order of God,
> In confident ignorance, but arrest disorder,
> Make it fast, breed fatal disease,
> Degrade what they exalt. (30)

The Third Tempter offers Thomas *future* prospects of greatness—by breaking faith with the king and siding with the wealthy barons. Many years after Becket's death in 1170, these same barons would indeed end Henry's "tyrannous jurisdiction" (33) by winning major political concessions from him through the Magna Carta that he and they signed in 1215. Again, there is a rough parallel between this temptation and the devil's offering for Jesus to rule over "all the kingdoms of the world and [to have] the glory of them" (Matt 4:8 KJV). Once more, Thomas remains rather primly righteous in his self-professed loyalty to the king:

> Shall I who ruled like an eagle over doves
> Now take the shape of a wolf among wolves?
> Pursue your treacheries as you have done before:
> No one shall say that I betrayed a king. (34)

Instead of ceasing with these three temptations that roughly parallel Christ's own encounter with the devil in the wilderness, Eliot presents a Fourth Tempter: one who is very clearly Satan himself. In the recorded version of the play, Eliot himself insisted on reading this part, and in some versions of the play Thomas actually joins voice with the tempter. The reason for this drastic shift is that, rather than being given easily-dismissed external enticements for avoiding martyrdom, Becket is now tempted by the subtlest of all evils: by his own *desire* to be killed and thus to be exalted in death as he is not celebrated in life. For while potentates rise and fall and are soon unremembered, saints and martyrs retain their fame despite the withering effects of time, both avenging foes and rewarding friends:

King is forgotten, when another shall come:
Saint and martyr rule from the tomb.
Think, Thomas, of enemies dismayed.
Creeping in penance, frightened of a shade;
Think of pilgrims, standing in line
Before the glittering jewelled shrine,
From generation to generation
Bending the knee in supplication,
Think of the miracles, by God's grace,
And think of your enemies, in another place. (38)

Eliot's rhymed couplets give incantatory force to this demonic voice that echoes Thomas's own hidden and unconfessed desire. Yet Becket soon confesses this subtlest of sins, in what have become the most celebrated (and also troubling) lines of the entire drama:

The last temptation is the greatest treason:
To do the right deed for the wrong reason. (44)

Here we are brought to a perplexing Christian paradox—that the highest and noblest act of faith can also become the worst act of sin. "For those who serve the greater cause [of God] may make the cause serve them, / Still doing right" (45). Martyrdom itself can be twisted from the supreme good into the supreme evil. This was a perplexity that the church faced early in its history, when Christians began *seeking* martyrdom, *wanting* to be put to death for the sake of their faith and thus for their instant translation into heaven. The church rightly ruled such acts to be selfish instances of suicide rather than true deeds of self-sacrifice. Suicide in turn was declared to be an instance of the sin of unbelief; i.e., the refusal to put our trust in the Holy Spirit to provide for us in cases of extremity, choosing instead to rely only on ourselves.

Self-immolating radical Islamists have made martyrdom a suspicious word in our own time. They blow themselves up in suicide bombings that destroy human life for the sake of their terrorist causes as well as for their own promised (and self-centered) entry into paradise. These Islamists have taken up a tradition that we Christians have largely abandoned—the notion that to die in defense of a righteous cause is to become a martyr. Mohammed himself is said to have wished for three lives in order that he might die thrice in defense of Islam, even though he strictly forbade suicide as a presumption upon the prerogative of God as the sole executor of both life and death. Yet it is doubtful that the pseudo-martyrdoms of Islamist extremists are the real reason Christians have largely abandoned dying as the ultimate form of Christian witness. The more likely reason is that we have accepted the secular and materialist gospel that life itself is the ultimate good. Hence our tendency to ridicule, as foolish and misguided, those who (like the young woman in the Columbine killings) died for their Christian faith. *Murder in the Cathedral* helps us to confront these difficult questions about what constitutes authentic martyrdom.

Eliot moves toward an answer to the vexing matter by having the Chorus succumb to the belief that, if Thomas dies, then the significance of their own lives will be lost. For if God's own archbishop can be slain by what Scripture calls "the governing authorities" that "have been instituted by God" (Rom 13:1), then surely the world is empty of ultimate worth and void of ultimate meaning—life itself being but what Shakespeare's Macbeth calls "a tale told by an idiot, full of sound and fury, signifying nothing" (act 5, scene 5), a universe whose godlessness both devours and mocks us. Their despair becomes a kind of spiritual suicide, a forsaking of all hope, thus pressuring Thomas to stay alive at all costs:

> The forms take shape in the dark air:
> Puss-purr of leopard, footfall of padding bear,
> Palm-pat of nodding ape, square hyena waiting
> For laughter, laughter, laughter. The Lords of Hell are here.
> They curl round you, lie at your feet, swing and wing through
>   the dark air.
> O Thomas Archbishop, save us, save us, save yourself that we
>   may be saved;
> Destroy yourself and we are destroyed. (44)

The lesson that Thomas must learn is the same lesson that he must teach the church; it is at once the simplest and most difficult of all lessons: the good but hard news that in our weakness lies our strength, that God chooses the foolish things of this world to shame the wise, that the cross is the supreme instance of such folly, and that God in Christ has (as the liturgy of the Eastern Orthodox churches puts it) "trampled down death by death." Thus is the meaning of life inseparable from the meaning of death, so that our living is also inseparable from our dying. The dramatically embodied teaching of *Murder in the Cathedral* is that martyrdom is but the ultimate form of the dying that Christians are meant to practice daily. The Christian life itself must be understood as a prolonged practice of dying before we die.

This is the real heart of Becket's sermon on Christmas morning of 1170, only four days before his death. It is clear that Thomas has now composed his mind and conformed his desire to the mind and desire of God. The Mass, he says, is a reenactment of Christ's own passion and death. It is rightly celebrated as the most hopeful of all events. The reason, as Eliot says in "East Coker," is that the Friday on which we humans did our worst possible deed—even as we blithely persist in slaying the incarnate God daily with our sins—has been transformed by this same God into the best of all days:

> The dripping blood our only drink,
> The bloody flesh our only food:
> In spite of which we like to think
> That we are sound, substantial flesh and blood—
> Again, in spite of that, we call this Friday good.[3]

Like Good Friday, Christmas is a time of simultaneous rejoicing and mourning. The coming of the Christ Child is also the occasion for King Herod's slaughter of the innocents; thus does the truly innocent One, because he threatens all coercive and domineering power, bring death to the totally innocent. The angels would seem, therefore, to announce an utterly false "Peace on earth." The earth's wars continue to rage, then as now. Yet there is peace to be found amidst this realm of endless death, Thomas declares. It is not the peace that means only the cessation of killing but rather the peace that refuses to kill at all, the peace that embraces the right kind of dying—the death, if the world would embrace it, that overcomes death:

> "Reflect now, how Our Lord himself spoke of Peace. He said to His disciples, 'My peace I leave with you, my peace I give unto you.' Did he mean peace as we think of it: the kingdom of England at peace with its neighbours, the barons at peace with the King, the householder counting over his peaceful gains, the swept hearth, the best wine for a friend at the table, his wife singing to the children? Those men His disciples knew no such things: they went forth to journey afar, to suffer by land and by sea, to know torture, imprisonment, disappointment, to suffer death by martyrdom. What then did He mean? If you ask that, remember that He said also, 'Not as the world gives, give I unto you.' So then, He gave to His disciples peace, but not peace as the world gives." (48)

II

Part 2 of *Murder in the Cathedral* rapidly works out the dire implications of Thomas's Christmas sermon. The Chorus no longer speaks in the plural but rather in the singular, as if to confess the sinfulness of their earlier attempt to dissuade Becket from martyrdom. It was wrong for them collectively to interfere with his vocation to death, and so the Chorus speaks as one person, each admitting guilt for having consented to the humiliating plea that Thomas flee from King Henry and his henchmen:

> I have smelt them, the death-bringers; now is too late
> For action, too soon for contrition.
> Nothing is possible but the shamed swoon
> Of those consenting to the last humiliation.
> I have consented, Lord Archbishop, have consented. (68)

The archbishop is surprisingly mild, even forgiving, in his response to the Chorus's confession. His explanation drives to the very core of Eliot's understanding of human and divine action in their proper relation. Thomas had voiced it earlier in response to the Chorus's call for him to avoid execution:

> They know and they do not know, what it is to act or suffer.
> They know and they do not know, that action is suffering
> And suffering is action. Neither does the agent suffer
> Nor the patient act. But both are fixed
> In an eternal action, an eternal patience
> To which all must consent that it may be willed
> And which all must suffer that they may will it,
> That the pattern may subsist, for the pattern is the action
> And the suffering, that the wheel may turn and still
> Be forever still. (21–22)

Eliot here strains language almost to the point of collapse, as paradox is laid upon paradox. The words are simple and plain but the meaning is exceedingly dark and difficult. What he seems to suggest is that we human beings are those finite and dependent creatures upon whom God acts through the joys and sorrows of earthly existence. Our lives are fundamentally to be understood in passive terms—as *patients*: God gives; we receive. Yet insofar as we learn rightly to accept and embrace these great and small events that lie beyond our ability either to compel or control, we also become *actors*, even contributors to the great turning wheel of time. God is no bully. God will not impose his will on the world. God abides in "an eternal patience," waiting with serenity and tranquility for our consent to that which he wills. God can remain "without shadow of turning" because he is the still point at the hub of things, the infinitesimally unidentifiable center who moves not at all while himself moving all things. Thus are suffering and action not opposites so much as complements within the divine order of the cosmos. The interwoven powers of action and suffering constitute reality itself.

Most of us want to escape this staggering paradox that requires both the right kind of action and the right kind of suffering *simultaneously*; we are eager, instead, to be either pathetic victims or valiant heroes. This unhappy fact brings Becket to make one of his most drastically misunderstood claims: "Human kind cannot bear very much reality" (69). This phrase is often interpreted to mean that God spares us from too great suffering lest we be overwhelmed and defeated by it. Yet this is not the case. The archbishop is stating exactly the opposite truth that we fear not pain and calamity so much as we dread the one abiding *reality*: the inseparability of gladness and suffering, the union of delight and death, the oneness of love and justice. For only through simultaneously painful and joyful moments do we enter eternity here and now, as the Third Priest makes evident at the very end of the play:

> Forgive us, O Lord, we acknowledge ourselves as type of the common
> man,
> Of the men and women who shut the door and sit by the fire;
> Who fear the *blessing* of God, the loneliness of the night of God, the
> surrender required, the deprivation inflicted;
> Who fear the injustice of men less than the *justice* of God;
> Who fear the hand at the window, the fire in the thatch, the fist in
> the tavern, the push into the canal,
> Less than we fear the *love* of God. (87–88; emphasis added)

Having grasped and held hard to this deepest and most difficult of all Christian paradoxes, Thomas has made perfect his will and is thus ready to be martyred—to do the right deed for the right reason. Entering the house of prayer and peace with swords drawn, four brutal and half-drunk knights—who have literalized King Henry's offhanded comment that he would like to be done with the interfering archbishop—come to kill

Becket. He insists that these murderous thugs not be barred from Canterbury cathedral, since blood has been "the sign of the Church always," and since complete obedience to the will of God marks the presence of eternal Love within the temporal muddle of good and evil:

> And as in time results of many deeds are blended
> So good and evil in the end become confounded.
> It is not in time that death shall be known;
> It is out of time that my decision is taken
> If you call that decision
> To which my whole being gives entire consent.
> I give my life
> To the Law of God above the Law of Man. (73–74)

The four knights begin immediately to excuse their savagery, in prose that might well be taken from the newspapers. Eliot wants us to see, as happened at the crucifixion of Jesus, that it is we ourselves and not only the Romans and Jews who killed Christ. The knights' excuses, like ours, are human—all too human—so pathetic in fact as to be comic, rather like the clueless soldiers casting lots for Christ's garments at the foot of the cross:

> When you come to the point, it does go against the grain to kill an Archbishop, especially when you have been brought up in good church traditions. . . . No one regrets the necessity for violence more than we do. . . . From the moment he became Archbishop, he completely reversed his policy; he showed himself utterly indifferent to the fate of the country, to be, in fact, a monster of egotism. This egotism grew upon him, until it became at last an undoubted mania. . . . Need I say more? I think, with these facts before you, you will unhesitatingly render a verdict of Suicide while of Unsound Mind. It is the only charitable verdict you can give, upon who was, after all, a great man. (79, 82, 83, 84)

Such will be the world's sorry verdict on Christian martyrs—that they are egoistic suicides. Yet Christians are not to be daunted by the slur. Whenever our witness scandalizes the world, it has at least been acknowledged as offering a drastically alternative way. The very wrongheadedness of the secular judgment pays unwitting tribute to Thomas Becket's chief teaching: the lordly Lover wounds his beloved that we might be made truly lovable; the heavenly Father chastens and disciplines his children that we might become Christian adults; the heavenly Vinekeeper cuts and prunes his vineyard that we might bear much fruit; the holy Jeweler refines his gold that it might be purged of all impurities; the sacred Potter smashes and refashions the clay of his earthen vessels that we might contain his transcendent grace and power, glory and peace—as Eliot himself declares in "Little Gidding":

> We only live, only suspire
> Consumed by either fire or fire.[4]

Ultimately, there are but two ways of life: to be devoured by our own hellish vanity and self-destruction, or else to be martyred to our own and the world's self-will.

HOSPITALITY AS THE GIFT GREATER THAN TOLERANCE IN G. K. CHESTERTON'S *THE BALL AND THE CROSS*[1]

"Modern toleration is really a tyranny," declares G. K. Chesterton. "It is a tyranny because it is a silence. To say that I must not deny my opponent's faith is to say I must not discuss it."[2] In a similarly barbed aphorism, Chesterton describes tolerance as "the virtue of a man without convictions." Chesterton thus explains the pagan persecution of the early church as oddly justified. Christianity, he says, "was intolerable because it was intolerant."[3] Such angular convictions often lead to the dismissal of Chesterton as an antediluvian reactionary seeking an ark whereon he might survive the flood of modernity, a comic curmudgeon vainly hoping to reinstate an idealized version of the Middle Ages.

Quite to the contrary, Chesterton was an unrepentant enthusiast for modernity's chief accomplishment—the French Revolution and its democratic deliverance of the common man from his old feudal estate as serf and villein, elevating him to a social and political sufficiency heretofore unknown. At last the world had recognized, in Chesterton's view, a fundamental teaching of the church that the church itself had often neglected. He affirms this teaching in his book on Dickens, that greatest of democratic novelists: "All men are equal as all pennies are equal, because the only value in any of them is that they bear the image of the King."[4] With democratic equality comes an attendant pluralism in matters political and religious, since neither the church nor the state can any longer exercise an externally imposed conformity to a single way of life. Instead, there are legitimate differences in both belief and behavior that the state must protect. The shorthand word for such a political regime is *liberalism*, and it is noteworthy that Chesterton styled himself as a Liberal (albeit as a member of a particular political party) from youth to death.[5] There are many kinds of liberalism, of course, but Judith Sklar describes the generic term quite adequately: "every adult should be able to make as many effective decisions without fear or favor about as many aspects of her or his life as is compatible with the like freedom of every other adult."[6] As a man who had made such an "effective decision" in becoming a Roman Catholic, Chesterton embraced the pluralism that enabled his open and public act. He crossed the Tiber, at least in part, because he sought a faith that would provide both pith and heft for the making of his literary witness in a democratic and pluralistic world.

That the religiously indifferent Chesterton first became a devout Anglican and then a Catholic convert indicates his early discernment that the liberal project would not suffice unto itself. It had a canker at its core, and the worm eating at its heart was called "tolerance." For while liberalism could offer protections against common evils, it would have an increasing difficulty defining common goods. Chesterton was among the first to recognize that his own inherited liberalism would issue in an unprecedented secularism, rapidly displacing religion from the center of human life.[7] The movement that began with the aim of setting people free would threaten, in fact, to empty the public sphere of those virtues that alone might prevent a return to the brute and slavish state of nature that Thomas Hobbes envisioned: the "war of all against all." Hence the need briefly to survey the history of tolerance and to outline a Christian alternative to it before embarking on a reading of *The Ball and the Cross*.

I

Toleration is a subject that, almost more than any other, preoccupies modern mentality. Baruch Spinoza, John Milton, G. E. Lessing, Pierre Bayle, Roger Williams, and William Penn all devoted themselves to it. Yet it is John Locke's "Letter on Toleration" that still shapes the debate. Once the Protestant Reformation had finally exploded the already disintegrating unity of Europe, repression and even civil war soon riddled English life. Having been religiously exiled to the Dutch Republic, where a secular state had been founded in order to permit religious differences, Locke sought to bring a similar freedom from religious persecution to his own nation. As himself a deist perched high above the religious fray, he sought to judge it from an ostensibly neutral perspective that credited only those universal ethical norms that all people of good will could discern.

The key to Locke's notion of toleration lies in his clear division between the civil and the religious realms: "He jumbles heaven and earth together, the things most remote and opposite, who mixes these two societies."[8] Our civil interests, as Locke defines them, are these: life, liberty, health, and property. Such public goods are construed as being external and thus as the proper realm of the magistrate or civil government. As such, they may and must be preserved by use of force, which is the government's chief legitimate power. Our religious interests, by contrast, are internal and private, for they concern salvation in the afterlife. The state has no power, therefore, to rule in this realm—to mandate the articles of faith, the forms of worship, or other religious disputes. For religion is not an outward and public but a private and individual matter. "The care . . . of every man's soul," Locke peremptorily declares, "belongs unto himself and is to be left unto himself."[9] Though he assumed that Anglicanism would remain the established state church, Locke urged that other expressions of Protestant religion should be tolerated, so long as they themselves remained tolerant. Yet two groups are not to be tolerated at all: atheists and Roman Catholics. Atheists deny the God who is the basis for the natural law that undergirds morality and the state.[10] Catholics are perhaps even more subversive to the commonweal of such a religiously pluralistic state. For they "deliver themselves up," Locke lamented, "to the protection and service of another prince."

The problem lies not with Locke's denial of state inducement of religious belief. As Locke rightly observes, God himself refuses to coerce people against their will. There are indeed religious requirements of both belief and practice that are mandated by the churches.[11] But the state has no such mandatory power over Christians. Such governmental force would prompt only empty outward conformity, not substantial obedience. Persuasion is the only legitimate means for inducing true faith. Even so, Locke remains the source of much of our mischief. The real trouble comes, in my estimate, when he excludes Catholics because of their allegiance to "another prince." He refers, in the literal sense, to the pope as a political figure allied with the various Catholic monarchs of Europe for political no less than religious purposes. Hence the common charge, if not necessarily the vile canard, that Catholics are "secret agents of the pope." Yet despite the example of Guy Fawkes, few orthodox Catholics, even in the late seventeenth century, would have regarded the papacy *primarily* as a political power unto whom they "deliver themselves up." On the contrary, they would have given him their allegiance as the earthly and religious representative of Another Prince, spelled in the upper case. Indeed, *all* Christians put themselves under the primary "protection and service" of this same Prince who is not the monarch or president of any worldly regime but Lord of the church. In the strict sense, therefore, Christians are subversive to *any* state that presumes to command the final loyalty of its citizens. For Locke, however, there can be no tournament of narratives, no hierarchy of loyalties between church and state, since heaven and earth constitute two societies that are inherently incomparable: they must not be "mixed."

Among the many problems arising from the Lockean idea of tolerance, William Cavanaugh has identified the most acute. He argues that toleration emerged as a means of halting the so-called "religious wars" of the seventeenth century no less as a political convenience than as a political necessity. According to Cavanaugh, these wars mark the birth pangs of the sovereign nation-state, with its massive growth in size and its increasing alliance with national and international markets. Political power was centralized, Cavanaugh argues, so as to provide "a monopoly on violence within a defined territory." Public discourse was deliberately secularized during the Enlightenment, Cavanaugh maintains, in order to save the state from the threat posed by the churches: "Christianity produces divisions within the state body precisely because it pretends to be a body which transcends state boundaries." The Enlightenment ideal of toleration thus excludes the communal body called the church, says Cavanaugh, "as a rival to the state body by redefining religion as a purely internal matter, an affair of the soul and not of the body."[12] In the name of an alleged inclusivity, therefore, a drastic exclusivity was promulgated. The state alone, not the church, can establish a true commonwealth, for religion now pertains chiefly to the private individual.

II

From such sentiments there emerges the modern individualism that values untrammeled liberty above all else—whether negatively defined as doing no harm to others, or else positively interpreted as constructing one's own life without let or hindrance. No longer is freedom understood as obedience to a *telos* radically transcending ourselves and thus wondrously delivering us from bondage to mere self-interest. Rather does liberty come to mean a life lived according to one's own individual construal of reality.[13] At its extreme, such individualism holds that we can make up our identity entirely out of whole cloth, that we can strip away all bothersome particularities that locate us within concrete narrative traditions, and that we can be free only as we rid ourselves of the troublesome commitments and obligations that we have not chosen entirely for ourselves. In sum, we may and must become autonomous selves, immunized from all moral and social obligations except those that we have independently elected.[14]

A crucial epistemological consequence is entailed by this privatizing and individualizing and subjectivizing of religion. The feminist political theorist Wendy Brown identifies it succinctly:

> [T]hat which is most vital to individuals qua individuals—personal belief or conscience—is not only that which is divorced from public life but that which is divorced from shared Truth. Tolerance of diverse beliefs in a community becomes possible to the extent that those beliefs are phrased as having no public importance; as being constitutive of a private individual whose private beliefs and commitments have minimal bearing on the structure and pursuits of political, social, or economic life; and as having no reference to settled common epistemological authority.[15]

There is also a drastic moral consequence inherent in this perspectival view of truth. Our late-modern notion of tolerance is usually advocated by those who have already attained such power that they can afford to "tolerate" their opponents—so long, it must be noted, as the tolerated abide by the rules laid down by the tolerators and thus offer no threat to established authority. Tolerance usually reveals that someone has already won and someone else has already lost. Our much-vaunted American ideal of state neutrality in religious matters often means that the governmental principalities and powers have already adopted a particular notion of the good built largely on Enlightenment and procedural notions of utility and rights.[16]

How, then, are those who hold to radically opposing construals of reality to deal with one another, if not by a polite tolerance that obscures the power arrangements underwriting it? Chesterton's *The Ball and the Cross* suggests that hospitality is a more excellent way. Hospitality of a Christian kind does not entail a smiling kind of niceness, a prim-and-proper etiquette, or even a gracious capacity for party giving. The word derives from *hostis*, a locution originally meaning not only "host" but also "stranger" and even "enemy." Hospitality thus becomes a Christian practice and discipline, a fundamental responsibility regarding those who are alien and perhaps even antagonistic toward us. It requires, among other things, the willingness to welcome the gift that others represent—not the gift that we expect or desire from them, but their often surprising and troubling gift, especially when others have convictions that are fundamentally hostile to ours. The word "tolerance," by contrast, originally meant "to endure pain or hardship," and it eventually came to signify "putting up with the opinions and practices of others." There is a decisive difference. *Tolerance* somewhat condescendingly declares that we will "put up with" others, even when their views and habits are noxious to us. *Hospitality*, by contrast, offers to "put them up" in the old-fashioned sense: we will make even our enemies our guests and thus our potential friends.[17] Hospitality thus becomes an earthly analogy to the gospel itself. Just as we were once strangers and enemies whom God has patiently taken into his household (Rom 5:10), so must we be willing to offer hospitality to those who are alien and hostile to us.[18]

Hospitality must not be romanticized and idealized as a simple or easy practice. It does not mean, for example, that we draw no distinctions among competing truth claims, as the proponents of tolerance often profess to do. Such subtle inhospitality actually despairs of the truth. If all truth claims are true, then none is true. As Chesterton was fond of saying, "morality is very much like art: it consists of drawing a line somewhere." Christian hospitality is willing to draw a line but not to raise a bar that cannot be crossed. On the contrary, gospel hospitality is willing to hazard two radical risks regarding opponents. On the one hand, it must take them so seriously that not only can they recognize themselves in our representation of their own most basic convictions but also that we ourselves must be susceptible of conversion to their faith. Yet on the other hand, we are also called to demonstrate the case for Christianity so persuasively in both act and argument that we help create the possibility of their conversion as well. In either case, we will not have merely tolerated each other: we will have exhibited the hospitality that eagerly engages the other.

III

The Ball and the Cross recounts the attempt of two vehement foes— one Christian, the other atheist—to have such an engagement. So important are their prime convictions that they have sworn not only to argue their ideas to conclusion but also to fight each other to the death in a duel with swords.[19] They are convinced that no belief is worthy of our life unless it is also worthy of our death. That this philosophical dust-up will take many surprising turns is indicated from the outset. Indeed, the central opposition is humorously set forth in the novel's opening scene. A professor named Dr. Lucifer has captured a Bulgarian monk named Michael from his mountain retreat and taken him aloft in his flying machine so as to demonstrate that the heavens are but a void and that the welkin rings empty of any divinity: "This mere space, this mere quantity, terrifies a man more than tigers or a terrible plague. You know that since our science has spoken the bottom has fallen out of the universe. Now heaven is the hopeless thing, more hopeless than hell" (2).* Rather stupidly mistaking the ball and cross atop St. Paul's Cathedral in London to be an actual planet, the professor almost crashes his spaceship into it. The monk takes the helm at the last minute and just barely avoids the collision, as Dr. Lucifer is recovering from his shock at seeing the cross for the first time, and thus having experienced a virtual exorcism!

Alison Milbank notes that Chesterton is seeking to destabilize his readers' imaginations, making the familiar London sight of St. Paul's into something no longer to be taken for granted but now made arrestingly strange.[20] The mime-like and semi-allegorical character of the novel is evident from the beginning. The monastic Michael possesses the faithfulness of the eponymous unfallen archangel, while the cleft-bearded Dr. Lucifer represents the mutinous archangel in modern form. That the monk and the professor begin a philosophical argument while clinging to the dome of St. Paul's indicates that we are not reading realistic fiction so much as deliberate farce. Why would Chesterton resort to a patently unserious genre such as farce, with its virtually impossible situations, its extravagant occurrences, its frantic pace and, above all, its wildly improbable conclusions? In a world becoming immune to the gospel, Chesterton believed that only those art forms that have the destabilizing power of farce and mime and even melodrama can capture the gospel's outrageousness, its fantastic eccentricity, indeed its scandalously joyful claim that God himself has entered the human fray in Jesus Christ and his church.[21]

---

*All quotations from *The Ball and the Cross* are taken from the Dover edition (New York, 1995) and are documented by page number within the text.

Farce also enables the creation of outsized characters who figure forth their representative beliefs in large and startling terms. The essential antitheses in *The Ball and the Cross* are embodied by an ardent English unbeliever named James Turnbull and a devout Scots Catholic named Evan MacIan: an urban Lowlander versus a rustic Highlander. They have come into conflict because MacIan has smashed the window of the editorial office at *The Atheist*, the journal that Turnbull edits. MacIan had been roused to wrath by Turnbull's article suggesting that the Virgin Mary is merely a mythical figure typical of all primitive religions—a pretty maiden who had consorted with a divinity and given birth to a hero. For MacIan, by contrast, she is the one about whom Christians make a staggeringly paradoxical claim—that this teenaged Jewish virgin is in fact the Theotokos, the very mother of God, the one whose womb bore the second person of the Trinity. She is the exemplary figure of Christian faith for having first professed belief in Jesus before he was even conceived. "Be it done unto me according to thy Word," Mary's faithful response to the Annunciation made by the archangel Gabriel, is indeed the profession that every Christian makes. Turnbull's blaspheming of the Blessed Lady, denying her uniqueness by reducing her to a mythic invention of the human imagination is, for MacIan, an act tantamount to denying Christ's own unique incarnation. These are fighting words indeed.

Yet nearly everyone in England is determined to prevent MacIan and Turnbull from having their fight. The alleged reason is that these men have pledged to conclude their theological debate with a sword duel unto death. Our tolerant and enlightened times, we are told, have advanced far beyond this benighted medieval practice. The main forces amassed against such a physical and metaphysical joust are journalists and the police. These two predominant shapers of modern life have been persuaded by "all the forward men of [the] age" (14) that dueling must be halted. Yet it is not chiefly the battle with blades that the establishment forces want to stop. Their covert aim is to prevent a serious argument.[22] Though the Enlightenment prized the debate of ideas and their consequences, Chesterton contends that the heirs of seventeenth-century argumentation have replaced philosophical engagement with a practicality and an efficiency that have been rendered all the deadlier by the absence of any aim or purpose beyond themselves. Broadmindedness has thus come to mean empty-mindedness, even if in unconscious rejection of Chesterton's tart aphorism: "The object of opening the mind, as of opening the mouth, is to shut it again on something solid."[23] Thus are the tolerant and "forward men of the age" unwilling to close their allegedly open minds even on a solid argument. On the contrary, they are determined to prevent Turnbull and MacIan from agitating the truly clamant questions concerning God and man and the world.[24] These idea-wranglers must be restrained not only from rapier thrusts but also from intellectual repartee.

It becomes evident that MacIan's argument with Turnbull is not about niggling niceties but about the most fundamental of all divisions: whether there is God, and thus whether there is man. The real issue, as MacIan discerns, is the relation of the ball and the cross atop the main dome of St. Paul's. Turnbull the atheist is devoted to nothing other than the earth. He is a moral man willing to make huge personal sacrifices for the sake of "honour," "liberty," and "humanity" (24).[25] He believes, however, that such high principles can be maintained without faith in God, in Christ, or in the church. The globe doesn't need the rood riding it. MacIan salutes Turnbull for dedicating himself to such worthy ideals, but he insists that they actually signal the death of man no less than the demise of God. Turnbull's humanistic values have no basis or sustenance, MacIan argues. They are cut off from transcendent reality, having no relation to any all-surpassing idea of the good. MacIan answers the modern attempt to finesse this most pressing of all questions by strongly defending the metaphysical goodness of things as the warrant for regarding human existence as having unique worth:

> "To me this whole strange world is homely [i.e., cheerful, warm, home-like] because in the heart of it there is a home; to me this cruel world is kindly, because higher than the heavens there is something more than humanity. If a man must not fight for this, may he fight for anything? I would fight for my friend, but if I lost my friend, I should still be there. I would fight for my country, but if I lost my country, I should still exist. But if what that devil [Turnbull] dreams were true, I should not be—I should burst like a bubble and be gone. I could not live in that imbecile universe. Shall I not fight for my own existence?" (19)[26]

IV

What "that devil" named Turnbull "dreams" is nothing other than the scientific physicalism[27] that has become the regnant (if unconfessed) creed of modern Western life. It is the notion that the universe is an unsponsored and undirected process, a self-sufficient realm of matter in motion, a domain having no ultimate aim or purpose beyond its own inherent patterns, so that nature exists only to be mastered and manipulated by human means for human ends alone. Everything that exists operates solely according to its physical nature and relationships. Physicalism is the philosophical air we all breathe, and it's all the more penetrating and suffocating for being so largely unconscious. Already in 1911, when *The Ball and the Cross* was first published, Chesterton had discerned that it would come to underwrite not only our thinking but also our entire culture of comfort and consumption. Its central though unstated premise is that the purpose of life is to stay alive as long as possible, the better to enjoy ourselves, often by means of hedonistic pleasures and sensate entertainments, or else to *improve* our physical existence by various methods of scientific hygiene.

Thus far the argument would seem to lie between theism and atheism, between a believer who credits the reality of God and an unbeliever who does not. Yet MacIan is no mere theist. He is a clandestine Thomist. He argues, therefore, that he consists of Form no less than Matter, and that the church is the place where his own bodily matter is given its proper form:

> "The Church is not a thing like the Athenæum Club," [MacIan] cried. "If the Athenæum Club lost all its members, the Athenæum Club would cease to exist. But when we belong to the Church we belong to something which is outside all of us; which is outside everything you [Turnbull] talk about, outside [even] the Cardinals and the Pope. They belong to it, but it does not belong to them. If we all fell dead suddenly, the Church would still somehow exist in God. Confound it all, don't you see that I am more sure of its existence than I am of my own existence?" (38)[28]

Here is the scandalous sticking point between MacIan and his atheist interlocutor. The absolute worth of human life is not to be found in matter alone but rather in matter as it is susceptible of form. As Chesterton will later declare in his splendid study of St. Thomas:

> [The word] formal in Thomist language means actual, possessing the real decisive quality that makes a thing itself. Roughly [speaking] when [St. Thomas] describes a thing as made out of Form and Matter, he very rightly recognizes that Matter is the more mysterious and indefinite and featureless element; and that what stamps anything with its own identity is its Form. Matter, so to speak, is not so much

the solid as the liquid or gaseous thing in the cosmos; and in this [conviction] most modern scientists are beginning to agree with him.[29]

MacIan puts his basic trust, it follows, in the all-decisive act of God to establish the final form of the world in the Jews and Jesus and the church. His essential identity issues from his baptismal life in the body of Christ. Odd though it seems to say, his humanity is something acquired no less than received; it flowers and flourishes only through its proper formation in the habits and practices of the Christian life. Far from being a cozy coterie of the likeminded, moreover, the church has taught MacIan to value strangers—even to honor enemies such as Turnbull—not with a condescending tolerance but with an engaging hospitality, if only in the oxymoronic hospitality of a sword fight! Hence the riotous irony of two would-be pugilists having to flee, by ever more outrageous escapes, from the forces of the law and the press.

> "I must kill you now," said the fanatic [MacIan], "because—"
> "Well, because," said Turnbull, patiently.
> "Because I have begun to like you," [answers MacIan]. . . .
> "Your affection expresses itself in an abrupt form," [Turnbull] began. . . .
> "You know what I mean," [MacIan continues]. "You mean the same yourself. We must fight now or else—"
> "Or else?" repeated Turnbull, staring at him with an almost blinding gravity.
> "Or else we may not want to fight at all," answered Evan, and the end of his speech was like a despairing cry. (37)

As the two enemies who are becoming friends escape both the press and the police who are trying to prevent their spiritual and bodily duel, they encounter two real enemies who, though initially eager to engage MacIan and Turnbull, finally refuse them hospitality. The first of these unwelcoming souls is a "Tolstoian" espousing a philosophy of universal peace based on an undiscriminating love of life. All sentient creatures have equal importance, he argues, so that cats and dogs and children are on a level plane, none to be exalted over the other. Physical suffering thus becomes the ultimate evil, since everything must be kept alive at all costs. To differentiate animals from humans is, in the ugly argot of our time, to be guilty of speciesism. Though Turnbull the humanist is appalled by this cosmic egalitarianism, MacIan the believer is almost persuaded by the Tolstoian's benign philosophy of "caring," so closely does it approximate the Christian desire to relieve misery. In his hospitable desire to "take in" other viewpoints, MacIan is himself almost "taken in." Suddenly an angel of light arrives to help MacIan drive out this demon of darkness who is a clear travesty of MacIan's own Christianity. Love, MacIan learns from the heavenly visitant, becomes wickedly saccharine if it is not rooted in the redemption wrought by authentic suffering:

> "'Give up fighting [the angel had told MacIan], and you will become like That [the Tolstoian]. Give up vows and dogmas, and fixed things, and you may grow like That. . . . You may grow fond of that mire of crawling, cowardly morals, and you may come to think a blow bad, because it hurts, and not because it humiliates. You may come to think murder wrong, because it is violent, and not because it is unjust.'" (44)

The more significant ideological devil is not the Tolstoian pacifist but a Nietzschean who is enamored of the will-to-power. His name is Wimpey and he is a hater of all humanitarianism. He worships naked strength and "Force"—the god who "loves blood" (52). Convinced that the universe is ruled by might alone, Wimpey hails what he calls "that naked and awful arbitration which is the only thing that balances the stars—a still, a continuous violence. Væ Victis! [*Woe to the vanquished! The conquered have no rights!*] Down, down, with the defeated! Victory is the only ultimate fact" (53). Turnbull begins to undergo a philosophical (if not yet a theological) conversion upon seeing that his physicalism has little means of answering Wimpey's kind of Nietzscheanism. It is grounded in a neo-Darwinian stress on "Nature loving the strongest" (55). Absent a vision of nature as ordered to the good of both humanity and divinity—mysterious and paradoxical though this order may be[30]—the Nietzschean will always maneuver a physicalist philosophy to his own maleficent purposes. It is altogether appropriate that he extend our contestants no hospitality, for the will-to-power is the only adjudicator in a world of unlimited perspectives.[31] Thus did Chesterton foresee that a softheaded tenderness and a cold-hearted hardness would become the chief modern enemies of atheism and Christianity alike.

Yet Chesterton does not allow MacIan and Turnbull either to flatten their opponents or to demonize each other, as if their own viewpoints were without flaws. "Idolatry is committed not merely by setting up false gods," Chesterton wisely observed, "but also by setting up false devils." The erstwhile combatants learn their limits after their last and most frantic escape leads them into the garden of an insane asylum. There MacIan and Turnbull experience nightmare visions of what the world would be like if their *own* philosophies were allowed to triumph unchecked. MacIan discovers that, if Christianity could be imposed upon others by force rather than persuasion, it would produce a cruel theocracy. Turnbull is shown something similar at work in a tyrannous version of his physicalism. His physicalist regime, he learns from his incubus, would first of all rid itself of "a hopeless slave population." As Stephen Clark has noticed, it is the poor who are "despised and murdered" under the iron fist of both Christian and atheist utopias,[32] but especially the latter: "No man should be unemployed. Employ the employables. Destroy the unemployables" (141). In a statement that would become the virtual motto for the twentieth-century culture of death, Turnbull's tormenting *Doppelgänger* proudly declares that "Life is sacred—but lives are not sacred. We are improving Life by removing lives" (141-42). MacIan learns that Christian conversion must never entail coercion, just as Turnbull finds that he must guard his physicalism against the manipulation of human life to anti-human ends. MacIan and Turnbull have both been radically humbled by their respective dream visions. They have discovered the truth of Chesterton's crisp dictum: "It is not bigotry to be certain we are right; but it is bigotry to be unable to imagine how we might possibly have gone wrong." Having been shown how dreadfully they might have gone wrong, MacIan and Turnbull are no longer bent on mutual slaughter—either by swords or squabble. On the contrary, they have become fast friends.

V

Yet their friendship is not confined to themselves alone. They are made to care for others when they discover the character of the mental institution where they have been locked away. It is a physically sanitized but morally monstrous place.[33] It has been established by a bill passed by the House of Commons mandating the imprisonment of everyone who cannot be medically certified as sane. This vast prison house of the allegedly mad contains, in fact, all of the truly sane people whom Turnbull and McIan have encountered during their flight, perhaps even all the remaining sane souls in England. The chief executive officer is, of course, Dr. Lucifer. He is determined to suborn the inmates into a willing cooperation with this giant bureaucratic scheme for preventing people from thinking seriously about their philosophy of life. Yet there is no worry that Turnbull or MacIan or anyone else might escape from the madhouse, for they would soon be arrested by the medical police and returned to the sanitarium: "In the first village you entered," they are told, "the village constable would notice that you were not wearing on the left lapel of your coat the small pewter S which is now necessary for any one who walks about beyond asylum bounds or outside asylum hours" (157).

This passage is remarkably prophetic. Chesterton saw, a quarter-century in advance, that democratic nations would soon begin branding their citizens with badges either of inclusion or exclusion.[34] Whereas in *The Ball and the Cross* it is those declared certifiably normal and balanced who are "rewarded" with an S, German Jews would soon be identified with white armbands featuring the blue Star of David. The first exclusion would bring spiritual, the latter literal, death. Lest Chesterton's fantastic caveat seem unlikely to be fulfilled—at least not in the all-tolerant nations of the modern West—it should be remembered that, only two years after the publication of *The Ball and the Cross*, Winston Churchill introduced the Mental Deficiency Act of 1913. It followed the Lunacy Act of 1890, which had given physicians virtual *carte blanche* in confining the allegedly mad to asylums.[35] Churchill proposed, among other things, that those lacking "sufficient" intelligence not be allowed to marry and thus not to propagate themselves. Yet the real animus was against the so-called "unproductive" poor. Chesterton was one of the few to recognize this scheme of ostensible social improvement as a demonic form of social Darwinism. It was but the final outcome of a savage kind of capitalism that was meant to trample the destitute and the pauperized, forcing them into self-abandoned drink and sex as their only earthly delights. Especially in his book, *Eugenics and Other Evils*, Chesterton inveighed mightily against this attempt to usurp divinity:

> It is not only openly said, it is eagerly urged, that the aim of the measure is to prevent any person whom these propagandists do not happen to think intelligent from having any wife or children. Every tramp who is sulky, every labourer who is shy, every rustic who is eccentric, can quite easily be brought under such conditions as were designed for homicidal maniacs.[36]

The question raised by *The Ball and the Cross* is whether we can still develop a public philosophy capable of resisting such eugenic evils. A recent Nobel laureate in physics, Steven Weinberg, suggests that we cannot. Weinberg has offered the morally self-canceling judgment that is but the latest version of unbridled physicalism: "The more the universe seems comprehensible," Weinberg has announced, "the more it also seems pointless." Weinberg urges his fellow physicalists, therefore, to take up arms against religion, routing all who would discern moral and spiritual order inherent in the way things are: "Anything that we scientists can do to weaken the hold of religion should be done," Weinberg urges, "and may in the end be our greatest contribution to civilization."[37]

The Ball and the Cross pushes readers to ask precisely Weinberg's question: whether a sometimes comprehensible but ultimately pointless universe can house and nourish anything akin to civilized life rather than the culture of death. Not even such a far-seeing prophet as Chesterton could have foreseen that ours would prove to be the deadliest era in human history, with more people killed by violent means in the twentieth century than in all the preceding centuries combined, roughly 180 million, most of them slain by their own governments. We can hardly expect a slender and farcical novel to provide a definitive answer to such an all-determining question. But at least it offers two crucial hints. The first comes by way of an outright miracle performed by Father Michael. Chesterton almost lets us forget the monk who had been imprisoned in the medical madhouse as a lunatic for claiming he landed in a flying ship. He has been confined to a lightless room having neither windows nor doors. The monk's tormentors had sought to increase his misery by giving his room irregular dimensions and by having a peg protrude from one of the cell walls, the better to remind him of their control over the meaning of things by way of this absurd projection.

Yet Michael has kept himself sane by touching and handling this seemingly meaningless spike. It sticks out from his prison wall precisely as the cross juts from the orb atop St. Paul's—not in mere usefulness but in a summons to redemption. Thus is the monk's soul confined but not killed, for he possesses the inner resources to keep himself spiritually sane amidst the total darkness, at least when such sanity is understood to accord with the foolishness of the gospel (1 Cor 1:18-30). Indeed, his soul has been transforming his mortal body so as to make it immortal and thus immune even to physical agony. As the asylum is being consumed by fires that threaten to incinerate them all, therefore, Father

Michael "walks through that white-hot hell . . . singing like a bird" (175). Approaching this apparent holocaust with both gladness and gaiety, the monk makes a path of deliverance for the inhabitants of this sanitized hell, much as Moses parted the waters for the Israelites so they might be released from bondage. We may require an apocalyptic miracle performed by an apocalyptic Saint Benedict or Saint Francis, Chesterton suggests, in order for our hell-and-death bent world to be rescued from its demoniac madness.[38]

Such an astounding miracle must be rightly perceived and truly embraced for it to have proper effect. Turnbull so receives and so embraces it, despite his miracle-denying physicalism. With one hand on the shoulder of the Christian woman he hopes to marry and the other on the shoulder of his newly acquired friend, the atheist Turnbull abandons the putative "certainties of materialism" (177) for the undeniable fact of Father Michael's walking through the separated flames. However reluctantly, Turnbull joins the others in falling to his knees.[39] Physicalism and Christianity are not here made complementary and thus necessary to each other.[40] The law of non-contradiction indicates that they cannot both be true. Indeed, the notion of the coincidence of opposites within a gigantic circle makes Chesterton sharply critical of Eastern philosophies.[41] Yet Turnbull's conversion is not won by either argument or miracle alone. He has also witnessed a strong if paradoxical kind of Christian hospitality at work in MacIan, the man who was once his worst enemy but who has become his most hospitable friend. Turnbull the humanistic atheist has also repeatedly befriended MacIan the unapologetic Christian. Chesterton suggests that atheists will be converted, and that Christians will cease being complacent and triumphalist, when they come commonly to discern the dreadful moral consequences of modern physicalism.

Yet the bonds uniting those who were once enemies unto death prove finally to be positive rather than negative. MacIan makes clear, in an earlier confession, that he is joined to Turnbull by the deepest of all human commonalities—the admission of his own sin as it is enabled by his own sometimes-sinful Christianity:

> "[A]ll England has gone into captivity in order to take us captive," MacIan confesses. "All England has turned into a lunatic asylum in order to prove us lunatics. . . . When I saw that, I saw everything; I saw the Church and the world. The Church in its earthly action has really touched morbid things—tortures and bleeding visions and

blasts of extermination. The Church has had her madnesses, and I am one of them. I am the massacre of St. Bartholomew. I am the Inquisition of Spain. I do not say that we have never gone mad, but I say that we are fit to act as keepers to our enemies." (167)[42]

"To act as fit keepers to our enemies" is not to seek victory over them. It is not to seek victory at all. In perhaps the novel's single most lapidary statement, MacIan declares, "The cross cannot be defeated because it is Defeat" (90). It is the Defeat that constitutes the only lasting Victory, the Foolishness that is the one permanent Sanity. MacIan and Turnbull were indeed mad in wanting to kill each other. They are saved not by tolerance, however, but by the hospitality that creates friendship. "A few days ago," MacIan again confesses, "you and I were the maddest people in England. Now, by God! I believe we are the sanest. That is the only real question—whether the Church is really madder than the world" (168).

The Ball and the Cross offers a powerful fictional demonstration that the mad earth requires the even madder cross, the instrument of suffering and shame that the incarnate God has transformed into the shape of Hospitality by mounting it himself, inviting all to bow before the ultimate act of divine humility.[43] "Turnbull," MacIan declares near the end, "we cannot trust the ball to be always a ball; we cannot trust reason to be reasonable. In the end the great terrestrial globe will go quite lopsided, and only the cross will stand upright" (168). False notions of tolerance, I have sought to show, often make the world wobble on its axis, producing alienation rather than reconciliation. Thus does the welcoming rood rightly crown the circling orb. It is not a knife thrust into the heart of the world, seeking to subjugate and tyrannize it. Rather is it a handle of hospitality set atop this bobbling buoy called the earth, so that all its floundering inhabitants might grab hold and be saved.[44]

CHAPTER SIX

DOUBT ABOUT THE GOODNESS OF GOD IN C. S. LEWIS'S *TILL WE HAVE FACES*

M any people assume that the chief question for our time is whether God exists. At unprecedented levels, Americans and Europeans are declaring that they are either non-Christians or atheists. It is indeed important to wrestle with the reality or else the unreality of God. Yet the quandary is not ended by answering either positively or negatively. In certain regards, atheists have an easier path than Christians. Once they have concluded that there is no God, they need not worry themselves over the problem of his nature—whether God is truthful or loving or just. Yet these are burning concerns for Christians. To have faith in God's presence in Israel and Jesus Christ and the church is also to wrestle with God's evident absence, apparent unconcern, and even seeming malevolence. The God who has revealed and identified himself as the just Creator and merciful Redeemer of the cosmos often takes on the features of the unthinkable: the God who is a Monster. Job protests that God has made his life miserable without cause. Jeremiah complains that God hides from us. The psalmist cries out, "How long, O LORD? Will you forget me forever? / How long will you hide your face from me?" (Ps 13:1). And thus does Jesus himself utter perhaps the darkest words of the New Testament, as he repeats Psalm 22:1 in his cry from the cross: "My God, my God, why hast thou forsaken me?" (KJV).

The question of God's goodness does not cease with Christ's resurrection and the coming of the Holy Spirit at Pentecost to establish the church as the people of God and thus as God's concrete witness in the world. On the contrary, many of the church's martyrs and saints have been buffeted by spiritual doubt, perplexed by intellectual contradiction, anguished by the malignancy of the world and by God's apparent refusal to remedy the trauma and torture experienced by millions of innocent ones. Martin Luther, Teresa of Avila, and John of the Cross are obvious examples, as are such eminent Christian writers as John Bunyan, George Herbert, and Gerard Manley Hopkins. Even Mother Theresa of Calcutta, perhaps the most notable saint of our time, confessed her overwhelming conviction that God had abandoned her and that he remained oblivious to her suffering for the sake of the poor. She was overcome, instead, with "just that terrible pain of loss, of God not wanting me, of God not being God, of God not really existing." Doubt seems intrinsic to God's holiest people, as if they could not believe in God's presence without also acknowledging his absence.

I

The narrator and principal character of C. S. Lewis's *Till We Have Faces* is plagued by similar doubts. She is a woman who stands at the center of Lewis's retelling of the Cupid and Psyche myth. Lewis sets his version of the story in the ancient European north soon after the barbarians have overwhelmed Rome but before they have been converted to Christianity. As its name perhaps suggests, Glome is indeed a gloomy realm. It is governed by Trom, a tyrannical king who is so ruthless and bloodthirsty that, when enraged, he stabs servants who displease him. In his mad desire for a male heir, he also slaughters women who fail to bear him sons. He coldly barters away his attractive daughters, moreover, as brides for rival kings. Orual is one of the king's unwelcome girl-children, but she is not a beautiful one. On the contrary, Orual has double cause for her complaint against the gods. Not only has she been born a woman in a cruelly patriarchal world, she has also been given an unsightly face—a visage so ugly, in fact, that her hair has been shorn like a boy's and she has been forced to wear a veil. Due to no failing of her own, therefore, Orual has been sentenced to a miserable life. Her narrative thus constitutes her lengthy diatribe against divine injustice.

Orual confesses that her existence has not always been miserable. There was once a bright and shining presence that gave joy to her life— one of the king's lovely female offspring named Psyche. From this delightful child's birth, Orual devoted herself entirely to Psyche's care, finding in her a worthy recipient of total sacrifice. As Psyche matured, their mutual love was strengthened by the presence of a third figure called the Fox. He is a Greek who has been captured and brought to Glome as a slave, then assigned the task of bringing rudimentary learning—especially writing and numbering—to the brutish and illiterate realm of Glome. The Fox is something of a Stoic in his conviction that the gods are no more than names for the forces of nature, and that the aim of human life is to put itself in accord with nature's impersonal but still moral powers. In today's terms, we might think of the Fox as a humanist having the craft of both tongue and vision that belongs to one who doesn't believe in the God of the Jews, the Muslims, and the Christians. Because he is no barbarian but a lover of noble things, the Fox becomes the natural tutor and friend of Orual and Psyche.

Yet there is a crucial point at which the Fox's Stoic philosophy clashes with Orual and Psyche's pagan religion based on sacrifices made to Ungit, a female deity who is roughly analogous to the Greek goddess Aphrodite and the Roman deity Venus. In one of the novel's most crucial scenes, Lewis tests his readers' powers of discernment by having the pagan priest of Ungit-worship make a vehement attack on the wisdom of the Fox's Stoic philosophy:

> "We are hearing much Greek wisdom . . ." said the Priest. "It is very subtle. But it brings no rain and it grows no corn; sacrifice does both. It does not even give them the boldness to die. . . . Much less does it give them understanding of holy things. They [the Greeks] demand to see clearly, as if the gods were no more than letters written in a book. I . . . have dealt with the gods for three generations of men, and I know that they dazzle our eyes and flow in and out of one another like eddies on a river, and nothing that is said clearly can be truly said about them. Holy places are dark places. It is life and strength, not knowledge and words, that we get in them. Holy wisdom is not clear and thin like water, but thick and dark like blood." (50)*

Our interpretation of this passage will govern much of our reading and appreciation of *Till We Have Faces*. On the one hand, Christians and Jews have spent much of their history trying to become disentangled from the propitiatory kind of religion that the priest embodies. The Jews abolished temple sacrifices, just as Christians regard Christ as the sole and sufficient sacrifice made by God on their behalf. Lewis makes us ask, therefore, whether Psyche was right to surrender her life in obedience to the notion that Ungit must be placated by human sacrifices. Once the deity's good will has been earned by such drastic religious payment, she believes, Glome will surely flourish.

---

*All quotations from Lewis will be taken from *Till We Have Faces* (New York: Harcourt, Brace, 1980) and are documented by page number within the text.

Lewis is dealing with a modern no less than an ancient problem. Much of popular Christianity is still beholden, alas, to the idolatrous idea that God rewards those who are sufficiently pious. From the beginning, the church regarded such human appeasements of the divine will as gross denials of the glad fact that God has become human in Christ so as to offer *himself* for our salvation rather than requiring us gracelessly to make remunerations in the form of either flesh or possessions. Thus far, it seems, the priest is dead wrong in exalting dark and superstitious blood over clear and reasonable water.

On the other hand, Christians have borrowed a great deal from the enlightened Stoics, especially from their ethics. The Stoics' stress on the virtuous life, their belief in the principle of godlike reason as directing the universe, their desire to regulate the passions—all of these proved so compatible with Christian teaching that they were adopted by the early church. Indeed, the Fox sounds almost like a Christian when Orual seeks his consolation after she thinks she has lost Psyche:

> "To love, and to lose what we love, are equally things appointed to our nature. . . . If we look at it [the loss of Psyche] with reason's eye and not with our passions, what good that life offers [human beings] did she not win? Chastity, temperance, prudence, meekness, clemency, valour . . ." (86)

Yet, lest we make any naïve identification of the Fox's Stoicism with Christian conviction, we must recall that, despite their occasional compatibility, they often contradict each other. For example, the Stoics regard the universe as uncreated and thus as itself divine. To give personal attributes to the Divine Nature—such as goodness and love—is to indulge in nonsense. "You might as well say the universe itched or the Nature of Things sometimes tippled in the wine cellar" (143). Stoics and Christians also honor differing kinds of death. Stoics fall on their swords when life becomes unworthy of living with dignity. Christians, by contrast, reject suicide as an act of presumption against the will and grace of God. If we are faithful, we will seek to die spiritually to our sins in order that we might live fully for God and neighbor, even though it may require our physical death.

Lewis is exceedingly subtle in setting up this opposition between the uncouth priest and the learned Fox. As the novel progresses, it becomes increasingly evident that both are necessary, though in different ways. Civilization could not exist without the Fox's learning and wisdom, since reason and order lie at the root of civilized existence. In the state of mere nature, life (as Thomas Hobbes famously observed) is "solitary, poor, nasty, brutish, and short." Even so, the priest's call to total bodily sacrifice entails a still deeper kind of wisdom, a truth closer to the gospel than is the Fox's Stoic humanism. Christian wisdom is indeed dark and thick with paradox. God's self-disclosure in the Jews and Jesus seems to constitute a staggering contradiction. How could the infinite God identify his purposes with a humble Semitic tribe? More unthinkable still, how could God become a finite and mortal man in Jesus of Nazareth, a little-known rabbi who suffered and died for our sake? These are dense and mysterious realities, not thin and self-evident ideas derived from reason alone. Already, therefore, we can discern that Orual will find her answer to the problem of suffering and evil, if at all, in a way of believing and living that is more akin to the priest's paganism than to the Fox's humanism.

II

When Psyche agrees to offer herself as a blood sacrifice to Ungit—giving herself to be devoured by Ungit's son called the Shadowbrute, a figure rather like the Roman god Cupid—in order that a terrible famine might be lifted from Glome, Orual is enraged. This act strikes her as rank superstition, for Orual has schooled herself in the Fox's Stoic view that the world is a gigantic self-enclosed process without beginning or end. Accordingly, even the most admirable sacrifice will have no effect on the inevitable course of things; we must simply resign ourselves to the unalterable patterns of natural cause and effect. (Here again, the Fox's philosophy is not far from the humanism of our own time.) Orual is even more deeply angered by Psyche's willingness to abandon Orual and all her other earthly loves for the love of Ungit. How, asks Orual, can Psyche give herself to a god whom she has never seen, in a sacrifice that has no guarantee of success, and with total disregard for her friends?

Psyche's response goes to the heart of the novel. She reminds Orual that she has always had a longing for death. It came upon her, not when she was most miserable and thus made to despair of remaining alive, but rather at the happiest times of her life, when she was walking on the hills with Orual and the Fox:

> "Do you remember? The colour and the smell, and looking across at the Grey Mountain in the distance? And because it was so beautiful,

it set me longing, always longing. Somewhere else there must be more of it. Everything seemed to be saying, Psyche come!" (74)

Here we encounter Lewis's notion of *Sehnsucht*, a German word that means a passionate longing, a lifelong homesickness, a perpetual desire that is itself more satisfying (as Lewis said) than any earthly fulfillment of it. The deepest gratifications of life leave us longing, Lewis insists, for something *more*—longing not for a repeat of some previously experienced ecstasy, longing not even for a more intense version of such earthly glory, but rather longing for the joy which, having once tasted and glimpsed it here and now, we know that we can behold and savor it only beyond the walls of the world. Thus do we pursue it for the rest of our lives.

It's important to note that Psyche's irrepressible desire to give herself to the gods, her conviction that they have chosen her ever since she was a small child in Orual's arms, her belief that life must be lived through a series of such surrenders: all these make her what Lewis elsewhere calls an *anima naturaliter Christiana,* a naturally Christian soul. Though Psyche lives in a pre-Christian time and realm, she has an instinctive sense that the purpose of life is to die rightly and faithfully, as we have seen Thomas Becket do in *Murder in the Cathedral.* Psyche understands intuitively that she is meant to serve as an expiation, a sacrifice made for the sake of others, and thus an offering that she cannot complete except by dying:

> "How can I be the ransom for all Glome unless I die? And if I am to go to the god [the son of Ungit], of course it must be through death. That way, even what is the strangest of the holy sayings might be true. To be eaten [by the god] and to be married to the god might not be so different . . .
> "... To leave your home, to lose you, Maia [i.e., Orual], and the Fox—to lose one's maidenhead—to bear a child—they are all deaths. Indeed, indeed, I am not sure that this which I go to is not the best" (72–73)

Life is a series of deaths, Psyche argues. For both good and ill, we are constantly required to give up the things we love. The question, as the novel makes clear, is whether we will surrender them faithfully and gratefully, or whether they will have to be wrenched away from us bitterly, even hatefully. Once she has given herself to the son of Ungit,

Psyche discovers to her surprise that he is not an all-devouring Shadowbrute like Ungit but a fierce and loving deity who takes the lovely Psyche as his bride. This surprising reversal of her expectations enables Psyche to explain the true nature of love to Orual: "You do not think I have left off loving you because I now have a husband to love as well? If you would understand it, that makes me love you—why, it makes me love everyone and everything—more" (158–59).

Psyche has learned the most important of all lessons: how to set her loves in order. By loving the god foremost, she can love all other things rightly. She loves them more rather than less, because she now understands *why* they are lovable: because, both in their limits and their possibilities, they have their existence only in relation to him. Thus can she love the Fox for his human wisdom, Orual for her sisterly care, nature for its great glory, the kingdom of Glome for its political and social order (minimal though it be)—but without worshiping any of them, since worship is due to Ungit and her son alone. This is a pagan way also of describing the very heart of the Christian life. To love God supremely is to avoid all idolatry. It is to seek first God's kingdom and righteousness, so that all the other good things might be given to us in their proper proportion and thus that they may be loved in their proper way.

Orual is not satisfied either with Psyche's teaching or her sacrificial act. On the one hand, she remains in her miserable state: both physically unlovely and personally scorned by her father the king. On the other hand, and worse by far, she is deprived of that daily protection of Psyche that had been the heartbeat of Orual's entire existence. Though Psyche's sacrifice has brought healing and prosperity to Glome no less than praise and glory to Psyche herself, Orual is resentful and suspicious. And so she decides to test the authenticity of Psyche's sacrifice: to find out whether Psyche really has been made the bride of Ungit's son, or whether in fact she was eaten by wild animals as she stood strapped to the tree of sacrifice on the Grey Mountain. Horribly, Orual hopes to find nothing there but Psyche's bones.

Orual prefers to discover Psyche dead and abandoned than for her to be alive and thriving in the house of the god—and thus no longer dependent on Orual's care. To her astonishment, Orual finds that Psyche was not killed but taken by the god as his bride, and that her free surrender to him has mysteriously brought the rains back to the parched land of Glome. Again, the allegorical link is not far to find: Christians are called the spouse of Christ, and our lifelong surrender to him is consummated in a paradisal life of incomparable beauty and peace called the marriage supper of the Lamb (Rev 19:9). This celestial realm intersects, moreover, with the created sphere, so that earthly miracles are strangely affected by human sacrifices and intercessions such as Psyche has made.

Yet Orual doubts the reality of Psyche's new home in the palace of the god. Though standing in the middle of it, she remains blind to its wondrous reality. Only once, when kneeling to drink from the river, does Orual get a glimpse of its glory: "solid and motionless, wall within wall, pillar and arch and architrave, acres of it, a labyrinthine beauty" (132). As soon as Orual stands up, her vision vanishes—as if her bent body indicated humility, whereas her erect posture indicates defiance. This infuriates Orual. To her, the gods have again proven themselves to be dark and mysterious when they should be plain and self-evident. Angrily and ever so poignantly, she protests the notion that she must live in two worlds rather than occupying only the Fox's static and self-referential universe. The ordinary world is as palpable as her own hand, yet this other and intersecting world is as numinous and para-doxical as Psyche's palace. Orual describes the clash of the two realms as "a sickening discord," "a rasping together of two . . . bits of a broken bone" (120).

> But . . . with the horror came the inconsolable grief. For the world had broken in pieces and Psyche and I were not in the same piece. Seas, mountains, madness, death itself, could not have removed her from me to such a hopeless distance as this. Gods, gods, always gods . . . they had stolen her. They would leave us nothing. (120–21)
>
> . . . And now, you who read, give judgment. The moment when I either saw or thought I saw the House [of Ungit's son]—does it tell against the gods or against me? . . . What is the use of a sign which itself is only another riddle? . . . They set the riddle and then allow a seeming that can't be tested and can only quicken the tormenting tool of your guess-work. If they had an honest intention to guide us, why is their guidance not plain? (133–34)

Orual's direct appeal to the reader brings us to the brink of decision. Can we credit another world than the one apprehended only through our five senses? Or is there also a supernatural sphere that constantly intersects it, calling us to discern the natural realm through the lens of transcendence, thus discerning wonders (and perhaps horrors) not available to the senses alone? This is Orual's question, but with a huge and dark difference. In her pre-Christian way, she believes that there are indeed gods and that they have created a beautiful world inhabited by lovely people. But she insists that these divinities are cruel, even hideous, in the demands they place on us. They play a cat-and-mouse game. They claim to desire our love and trust and obedience, yet hide and disguise themselves so fully that we can never know whether they are real or illusory. They demand that we give ourselves to a reality that cannot be proved to exist. Worse still, they allow us to suffer inconsolable personal losses, whether by accident, by disease, or by betrayal. Worst of all, the gods do not merely *permit* our anguish but actually *cause* it. They win the love of those whom we cherish as our own. Thus are our dearest ones "stolen" in this precise way: they come to love and trust and obey divinity even more than us. Orual is no mere atheist, therefore, but a bitter anti-theist: she hates and despises these love-robbing gods.

III

The remainder of the novel can be summarized briefly in order to arrive at the surprising answer that Orual finally receives. Rather than permanently lose Psyche to the love of Ungit's son, Orual resorts to a desperate ploy: she demands that Psyche gaze upon the god who has become her husband but who has commanded her never even to glimpse him. Mortals cannot look upon immortals, so hugely do they differ in kind, not only in degree. The gods are holy and pure; we humans are frail and fallen dust. Psyche refuses Orual's order, of course. Then Orual plays her truly sinister trump card: she threatens to thrust a dagger into her own heart if Psyche does not light a lantern and behold the son of Ungit. In a terrible sense, the ploy works. No matter how fierce her punishment, Psyche prefers to violate the will of the god in pity for her sister, rather than to let Orual die in sure damnation for her act of self-murder.

Not only does Psyche surrender her privileged life in the Son of Ungit's palace by observing him; she is also sentenced to a harsh exile for her deed. In one of the novel's most remarkable scenes, the god himself appears in order to judge both Psyche and Orual. To have the divinity show his face and actually speak is a virtually impossible task, lest he look and sound like a mere man; yet Lewis magnificently, if also mysteriously, succeeds:

A monster—the Shadowbrute that I and all Glome had imagined—
would have subdued me less than the beauty this face wore. And I
think anger (what men call anger) would have been more supportable
than the passionless and measureless rejecting with which it looked
upon me. . . . He rejected, denied, and (worst of all) knew, all I had
thought, done or been. . . .
     The thunder had ceased, I think, the moment the still light
came. There was great silence when the god spoke to me. And as
there was no anger (what men call anger) in his face, so there was
none in his voice. It was unmoved and sweet; like a bird singing on
the branch above a hanged man.
     "Now Psyche goes out in exile. Now she must hunger and thirst
and tread hard roads. Those against whom I cannot fight must do
their will upon her. You, woman, shall know yourself and your work.
You also shall be Psyche." (173–74)

The final sentence is one of the most mysterious in the entire novel.
We learn, on the one hand, that Psyche will confront savage tasks, just
as Orual will face the ferocious consequences of her sin. Both of them
thus shall suffer. What does it mean, on the other hand, for Orual *to be
Psyche*? Does it mean that she shall undergo the same arduous exile as
Psyche? After all, Orual seems set for divine banishment. Or does it
mean something staggeringly paradoxical—that Orual shall become as
beautiful and faithful as Psyche? This seemingly impossible possibility
constitutes the pith and marrow of *Till We Have Faces*.

At first, Orual's doubts about the gods seem vindicated. While she
veils herself in shame for her violation of Psyche's trust, the mantle
invests her with an air of mystery that makes the people of Glome mar-
vel. With the aid of the Fox and especially with the help of her right-
hand man named Bardia, Orual brings great progress to her realm.
Determined "to drive all the woman out of me" (184) she rules her
realm like a hard-willed king. She widens and deepens the River
Shennit, increases the level of learning in Glome, and even defeats the
rival King of Phars in personal combat. Rather than languishing in failure and defeat, therefore, Orual thrives in victory and prosperity. "If
Orual could vanish altogether into the Queen," she muses, "the gods
would almost be cheated" (201). To do what the gods declare to be evil
is not to be punished, it seems, but to succeed.

Again, we are confronted with an ancient perplexity. Why do the
wicked thrive and the righteous suffer (see Ps 73:12-14)? Lewis answers
this perpetual problem less with philosophical arguments than by

revealing that evil wreaks misery upon itself. Though Orual would seem to be triumphant in her defiance of the gods, she gradually becomes unable to hear the voice of Psyche weeping, having lost her chief virtue of pity. She also cares ever less for the dying Fox, as she withers into a lonely solitude bereft of friends. Orual also discovers, to her horror, that she has demanded such devotion from Bardia that she has consumed all his energies, leaving nothing for his wife. Worst of all, she finds that she is left with a massive inward emptiness, as if she had performed a spiritual abortion on herself, a reverse gestation, killing her capacity to produce life, unable to care about anyone but herself. Orual's lament sounds all too much like the confession of Americans who are driven by relentless work and the desire for power and prestige, only to find that it's all a futile game:

> I did and I did and I did—and what does it matter what I did? I cared for all these things only as a man cares for a hunt or a game, which fills the mind and seems of some moment while it lasts, but then the beast's killed or the king's mated, and now who cares? It was so with me almost every evening of my life; one little stairway led me to feast or council, all bustle and skill and glory of queenship, to my own chamber to be alone with myself—that is, with a nothingness. (236)

Hoping to fill the huge void that causes her spiritual ache, Orual undertakes a "progress," a regal tour of the far-flung kingdoms she has conquered and annexed to Glome, the better to convince herself that her many triumphs prove that she really has succeeded in cheating the gods. Yet no matter how distant the land, Orual finds the same recurring and disturbing pattern: the sacred story of a maiden who offered herself as a sacrifice to a god. The deity found the girl so beautiful that he married her, taking her away to his secret palace to dwell there on the condition that she not look upon him. But then when the maiden's sisters came to behold the palace, they were so inflamed with jealousy that they sought to destroy their god-favored sibling. She in turn was exiled and made to undertake terrible tasks. Though weeping and wandering for many years, the blessed bride finally completed her arduous labors and was reunited with her husband, becoming a goddess alongside him.

Immediately after completing her royal tour, Orual sets about writing her diatribe against the goodness of the gods. Having heard the same "sacred story" repeated in several different ways, Orual sees that it's her own story and that it implicitly indicts her for having been *jealous* of Psyche's glorious state. Orual believes, on the contrary, that her relation to Psyche was based entirely on love and care, never on envy or resentment. Yet why should the Psyche story persist, even in the most far-flung regions of her realm? Here again we are confronted with another crucial point of interpretation, another instance of Lewis's conviction that pagan religions often anticipate Christian revelation.

Lewis learned from his friend J. R. R. Tolkien that many of the pagan poets and religions should not be regarded as enemies, although some of them, at their worst, assume that human beings must arduously earn their own salvation by placating the wrath of the gods. Yet at their best, they are examples of humanity's "good dreams." They constitute far-off longings and anticipations of the gospel. The gospel story does indeed resemble the mythic patterns found in many pre-Christian cultures, especially those centered upon dying and rising gods; for they too are built on the centrality of divine sacrifice. Yet there is a tremendous difference, Tolkien argued. The gospel story actually happened; myth became history. God himself has taken human form, dying in our stead at Golgotha. Yet the ultimate miracle is not only that God bodily raised the crucified from death, but also that, in so doing, God historically fulfilled humanity's profoundest desire. Christ comes not, therefore, to crush and destroy these salutary foretastes of God's true will for the world, but rather to complete and fulfill them by way of their total transformation.

The religion centered on the goddess Ungit is one of these mysteriously prospective versions of the truth, a distant gleam of the gospel in primitive pagan shape. The Cupid and Psyche myth, as here retold by Lewis, is an even larger mythic version of the gospel. Having sacrificed herself to the god of love, not for the sake of her own reward, but to bring good to her people, Psyche finds lasting favor with this god as well as atoning for the sins of her jealous siblings. The parallels with Jesus are unmistakable. Yet Psyche is no Christ, no unique and definitive incarnation of the triune God. She is a mortal woman who is made morally and spiritually complete through her total and trusting obedience.

In the Eastern Orthodox tradition, *theosis*, or divinization, is regarded as the chief aim of Christian existence. We are meant to be *perfected* in Christ even as he is perfect in the Father (Matt 5:48). Hence Psyche's many likenesses to the ideal Christian—her loveliness of character, her obedience of will, her submission to undeserved suffering for the sake of others. Orual, in turn, is a figure of quintessential sinfulness. She is no ogress of evil, however, for she does not secretly calculate how she might accrue divinity unto herself. Exactly to the contrary, Orual becomes sinful in her self-giving devotion to Psyche. She corrupts the highest of virtues (humble love of another) into the worst of vices (proud love of herself). Having rescued Psyche from loneliness and perhaps even death, Orual wants to possess Psyche solely as her own. Thus does she exemplify the most basic Christian teaching about evil: it cannot stand alone in its own sufficiency but exists always and only as a perversion of the good. Orual has twisted and corrupted the good of self-surrender into the evil of self-seeking.

IV

Part 2 of Till We Have Faces is Orual's brief but rending admission of this terrible truth. She has learned the nature of her own sinfulness, ironically, by composing her sinful attack on the gods. Their refusal to answer Orual's complaint has become the surprising means of her self-discovery. Their unrevealing silence has led to her revelatory speech. Writing is a necessary art because it enables both communication with others and also detection of our own spiritual state. We may gain unwanted self-knowledge by reflective articulation even of seemingly legitimate complaints. As Saint Augustine observed, "I must confess that, personally, I have learned many things I never knew before . . . just by writing." "It was a labour of sifting and sorting," Orual adds, "separating motive from motive and both from pretext" (256). Having abhorred Ungit as the greedy goddess who swallows up human lives, Orual discovers that she has become the very thing she abhorred: "It was I who was Ungit. That ruinous face was mine. I was that . . . all-devouring womblike, yet barren, thing. Glome was a web—I the swollen spider, squat at its center, gorged with men's stolen lives. . . . I was Ungit; I in her, and she in me" (276, 288).

Now, at last, Orual understands why the people of Glome worshiped her as their jealous god no less than as their forceful queen. In an appalling reversal of the gospel (compare Gal 2:20 and John 15:4), Orual became an embodiment of Ungit. This is a horrifying disclosure, for it reveals Orual to have been not only humanly but divinely rapacious in her desire to dominate Bardia and Psyche. Completely overwhelmed by her guilt, Orual decides to destroy herself by drowning in the River Shennit. Yet just as she is ready to plunge to her watery death, a voice calls to her. Again, Lewis accomplishes the virtually impossible by having divinity speak convincingly, this time in mercy rather than judgment:

> A voice came from beyond the river: "Do not do it."
>   Instantly—I had been freezing cold till now—a wave of fire passed over me, even down to my numb feet. It was the voice of a god. Who should know better than I? A god's voice had once shattered my whole life. They are not to be mistaken. . . . No one who hears a god's voice takes it for a mortal's.
>   "Lord, who are you?" said I.
>   "Do not do it," said the god, "You cannot escape Ungit by going to the deadlands, for she is there also. Die before you die. There is no chance after." (279)

The Christian implications of this scene are enormous, though conveyed under pagan guise. First, there is the revelation of Orual's sin. She discovers it not only by her own powers of self-analysis but also as it is divinely shown to her. It is noteworthy that Orual uses the personal form of address, calling the invisible "god" by his divine name: Lord. What the divinity shows her are not her various and individual sins but rather her fundamental condition of Sinfulness. The distinction between Sin in the singular and sins in the plural is enormous. The word *sins* describes the many evils, whether great or small, that we commit because we inhabit the ancestral state of *Sin* spelled in the upper case. *Sin* is our disease, our utter alienation from God. Luther likened it to leprosy, noting that this dread illness cannot be cured "pustule by pustule."

Christ's saving sacrifice on the cross is thus the remedy for the contagion of evil. Rather than having us strive vainly to overcome this or that failing (i.e., particular sins), we are meant to become God's own righteousness—the reformed and transformed people called the body of Christ.

But of course Orual the pre-Christian cannot know Paul's teaching that God subjected the sinless Christ to the whole burden of human sinfulness in order that its crushing weight be lifted from us (2 Cor 5:22). Seeing only that she dwells in the fatal state of Sin, Orual decides to kill herself in despair over any hope of redemption. Yet just as Sin must be disclosed to us from beyond ourselves, so must its cure be transcendently delivered. Hence the saving message from the god who will not let her die until she dies. Clearly the divinity refers to death in two senses rather than one. Before Orual dies literally in her mortality, she must die spiritually in her heart and will. She will go to her grave in utter misery unless she learns first to die to her massive self-seeking—laying it down, giving it up, surrendering it all.

Yet this fresh signal of hope quickly withers, as Orual immediately perceives that, of her own powers, she cannot undertake such radical renovation. She is indeed sick unto death with her own sinfulness, and she will soon die of it. If the revelation of her deathly condition must come from the gods, as we have seen, so must its remedy. And yet the gods remain silent once more, refusing to offer Orual the help she desperately needs. In a dream vision, however, Orual sees that she has indeed been provided such aid, ever so mysteriously, by a human mediator of divine grace: Psyche. For Psyche has performed all of the fiercely hard tasks that were meant for Orual, sparing her from having to accomplish them herself. Indeed, Psyche has carried the sorrows that Orual so fully and terribly deserves. But because Psyche bore these burdens gladly, they became occasions for delight rather than grief, as Orual now sees: "She won without effort what utmost effort would not win for me" (284).

The second truth Orual learns is that the anguish she had interpreted as the wrath of the gods was in fact the result of their carefree exuberance, their frolicsome playfulness, as she acknowledges in a cryptic affirmation: "the Divine Nature wounds and perhaps destroys us merely by being what it is" (284). Orual has learned from the Fox that God and Nature cannot be separated, and that life heedlessly tramples us with its heartaches and diseases and finally with death itself, stripping us of all notions of self-sufficiency. Lewis himself does not collapse Nature with Divinity, but neither does he envision them as separate spheres impermeably sealed off from each other. Instead, he holds that God works *within* the natural order rather than magically interrupting it on our behalf at every moment of danger. God *uses* the natural sorrows that are endemic to human existence for our good by turning them into potential blessings rather than curses. To be thus wounded is, rightly understood, a painfully paradoxical gift.

Yet divine action is not limited to such indirect uses of suffering. God himself intervenes for our salvation, demanding that, like Jacob and Job, we confront him directly. "You shall be Psyche" is a divine promise that reveals this second and more decisive form of redemption. Orual must be identified with Psyche not chiefly in her temporal misery but rather in her eternal joy, not so much in physical repugnance as in spiritual beauty. An awesome exchange thus occurs between Psyche and Orual. It is a substitution very much akin to the atonement that Christ enacts for the sins of the world. Though himself sinless, Jesus was made "to be sin . . . so that in him we might become the righteousness of God" (2 Cor 5:21). Once again, Psyche does not function *as* Christ, as if her sacrifice were meant for the salvation of the whole world. But she does serve as the novel's Christ-figure, one who reveals the nature of the Christ who is unknown to Orual. Indeed, Psyche makes Orual's salvation possible by putting herself in Orual's place, suffering the evils that were meant for Orual herself. Thus has Orual indeed *become* Psyche.

One thing needful remains, a requirement that no one can satisfy but Orual herself. She has been provided the necessary aid, in both human and divine form, for "dying before she dies"—laying down her ingrained sin in order that she might be resurrected to newness of life. Orual needs to utter but one single-syllable word, and yet it proves to be the most demanding word of all. This little three-letter vocable, precisely because it must be wrenched from us, is also C. S. Lewis's answer to the problem of doubt and suffering. The terrible and ultimate difficulty is not that God is grotesque, as Orual once had thought, but that God is beautiful beyond all resistance. Though we allegedly despise and reject God because he *permits* unnecessary suffering, the greater reason for our unbelief, Lewis demonstrates, is that God *demands* necessary suffering. God will wrench from us all those loves, however noble, that are not ordered to the love of God. God is determined to make us beautiful (i.e., joyful and faithful) by transforming our blighted condition (i.e., our reliance on other things). Yet, like Orual, we prefer our own ugliness to the divine loveliness, as she declares in a final outburst:

> "Do you think we mortals will find you gods easier to bear if you are beautiful? I tell you that if that's true we'll find you a thousand times worse. For then (I know what beauty does) you'll lure and entice. You'll leave us nothing; nothing that's worth our keeping or our taking. Those we love best—whoever's most worth loving—those are the very ones you'll pick out. Oh, I can see it happening, age after age, and growing worse and worse the more you reveal your beauty: the son turning his back on the mother and the bride on her groom, stolen away by this everlasting calling, calling, calling of the gods. Taken where we can't follow. It would be far better for us if you were foul and ravening. We'd rather you drank their blood than stole their hearts. We'd rather they were ours and dead than yours and made immortal. . . . That there should be gods at all, there's our misery and

bitter wrong. There's no room for you and us in the same world. You're a tree in whose shadow we can't thrive. We want to be our own." (290–91)

In pre-Christian form but deeply Christian substance, Lewis confronts his readers no less than his protagonist with the ultimate question: whether we will seek to keep ourselves and those whom we love most as our own property, or whether we shall surrender both them and ourselves as belonging to God and thus meant for his good keeping. "The one principle of hell," Lewis liked to quote his spiritual mentor George MacDonald, "is 'I am my own!'"[1] To be her own is what Orual desperately desires. This, alas, is the real source of her uncomeliness: she is not physically so much as spiritually disfigured. Yet the triune God cannot and will not behold such ugliness of soul, lest his beauty destroy us. God requires only that we speak a single word:

> When the time comes to you at which you will be forced to utter the speech which has lain at the center of your soul for years, which you have, all that time, idiot-like, been saying over and over, you'll not talk about the joy of words. I saw well why the gods do not speak to us openly, nor let us answer. Till that word can be dug out of us, why should they hear the babble that we think we mean? How can they meet us face to face till we have faces? (294)

Here we have not only the title but also the climax of the novel. Though never overtly spoken, the requisite word remains evident. It is simply and yet profoundly the word "Yes." This is the deepest of all utterances, this singular assent to the terrible goodness of God, this word that every four-year old and every grizzled adult can pronounce. We have no face until we face God by answering with this great and glad *Yes.* We thus acquire our faces—our identity, our character, our hearts and souls, indeed our very lives—as they are meant to be. The ancient Greeks called a slave by the name *aprosopos:* one who has no face. "When souls start to break down," wrote Nicholas Gogol, the eminent Russian novelist of the nineteenth century, "then faces also degenerate."[2] Ours is an age of deteriorating faces, largely because we have lost sight of the face of God disclosed in Jesus Christ. In *Till We Have Faces,* C. S. Lewis has given splendid fictional embodiment to this most astonishing answer to the problem of evil and doubt. It is we ourselves who, in our evil acts, should be doubted as having any right to be called human. Yet God will not countenance our disfigured countenances, even though we flee into the hellish depths of our own ugliness. God is determined to make us beautiful, in order that we might behold him face to face, but also that we might behold all the other saints who have thus acquired their transfigured faces, so that together we might share the blessed and eternal life.

CHAPTER SEVEN

CHRISTIAN LIVING TOWARD THE END OF TIME IN WALTER MILLER'S *A CANTICLE FOR LEIBOWITZ*[1]

We often misinterpret the doctrine of eschatology and the four last things—death, judgment, heaven, and hell—as if they had to do only with life beyond death. On the contrary, the early Christians believed that Jesus brought an end to the old Evil Age and that they were living in the New Era. These first believers were right. Christ has "trampled down death by death," as the great hymn of the Eastern Orthodox Church puts it. He has already established his kingdom in and through his church, enabling Christians, not to focus their lives primarily on some future state beyond the bounds of time and space, but rather to live out the mandates and promises of the gospel here and now. We should properly speak, therefore, not of "life after death" but rather of "life after life after death." Since Christ has already overcome death, we are those who have been raised from death and thus who are already participating in his New Life.

The *End* will surely come when the Lord shall indeed return—making a final division between the sheep and the goats, the good and the evil ones; but also bringing a *new* heaven and a *new* earth, where there will be no more tears and where sin shall reign no more. Yet this New World will not abolish the old so much as it will complete and perfect what Jesus has already begun: "Thy kingdom come, Thy will be done, in earth, as it is in heaven" (Matt 6:10, KJV). The hour and place and manner of Christ's coming are entirely of *his* knowing and doing, not of ours. It is idle speculation and even faithless distraction, therefore, to be obsessed with such things, as if the Christian life were primarily an affair of rewards for us and punishment for our enemies. What we *can* know and do, however, is to live expectantly toward this great culmination. A right regard for heavenly things, it follows, is the surest way to cultivate a right regard for earthly things. We will live redemptively here and now precisely as we remain focused on the kingdom that is already come and yet still coming. This is an especially important reminder, particularly during a terrorized time such as ours, when mass, even global, destruction seems already at hand. Walter M. Miller Jr.'s *A Canticle for Leibowitz* offers inspiring, if also frightening, guidance for living in the presence of such a holocaust.

The strange power of *Leibowitz* is hard to define. It is not a conventional work of science fiction, despite its obsession with technology, since most of its action and characters are quite realistically depicted. Neither is it a dystopian novel in the fashion of George Orwell's *1984* or Aldous Huxley's *Brave New World*, though it certainly depicts a nightmarish future. I believe that it should be read, instead, as an apocalyptic work. Even here qualifications are necessary. It is not apocalyptic merely because it concerns the culmination of things in an atomic holocaust. Rather it is an *apocalypsis* in the literal sense: an "unveiling," a revelation of the deeply destructive urges at work in late modern life. Miller has reverted to an ancient literary form in order to make radical religious claims. Yet like the apocalyptic books of the Bible—Daniel, Ezekiel, and Revelation itself—*Canticle* is much more than a warning of the wrath to come: it also offers a psalm of praise to the hope that might yet rescue the world from its otherwise fatal forgetfulness.

The book is set in the American Southwest, and it falls into three sections: *Fiat Homo* (Let There Be Humanity), *Fiat Lux* (Let There Be Light), and *Fiat Voluntas Tua* (Thy Will Be Done). The three plots unfold in the third and fourth millennia, many centuries after our present world has been wasted in a nuclear bonfire. In the novel's first section, barbarism still reigns. Tribal chieftains operating from their lairs in Denver and Laredo and Texarkana make constant warfare on one another. In the book's middle division, the rudiments of scientific learning have been recovered in the kingdom of Texarkana and are being developed in the service of a secular state. In the book's concluding part, this renewed science has produced nuclear weapons that are at last unleashed in yet another example of Mutually Assured Destruction. It is not difficult to discern that Miller has created an allegory that roughly recapitulates the last fifteen hundred years of Western history: the triumph of barbaric violence with the destruction of the Roman Empire, the rebirth of learning during the Middle Ages and the Renaissance, and then the terrible destruction that has befallen the modern world by means of secular science.

What gives the novel its artistic unity and thematic power as a true apocalypse—an unveiling of the truth about how to live in a world such as ours—is the Order of the Blessed Leibowitz. This small band of Christian monks is named after its founder and martyr, Isaac Edward Leibowitz. He was an electrical technician who had been an enthusiast for nuclear power until his wife was killed by radioactive fallout following the *original* twentieth-century atomic incineration. The drastically humbled Leibowitz then founded a monastic community in repentance for such a dread deed. This order of monks, now living two millennia later, refer to the first nuclear bonfire as the Flame Deluge, the firestorm that parallels the devastation wrought by the ancient Water Deluge involving Noah and his ark. Their phrase also evokes comparison with the destruction prophesied in Revelation 15:8-9, when the wrath of God scorches men with fierce heat.

Yet neither the mythical Genesis flood nor the modern atomic bonfire is to be confused with the final Apocalypse, for the former were both massively destructive, while the last will be a divinely creative event. The monks of Blessed Leibowitz are seeking to prepare themselves and the world for this true culminating End when God will make all things new and whole. They know that God's kingdom will not come on earth without the renewal of the human mind and human culture, no less than the human heart. And so they seek to keep alight the tiny lamp of learning within their new Dark Age that is all too much like our own.[2] These holy men have thus become copyists, memorizers, and *bookleggers*. They smuggle manuscripts. They copy and illustrate and commit them to memory, preserving the small scraps of human culture that remain. Nothing written, they believe, can be entirely worthless.

In their patient and thankless work of preserving knowledge, the monks set themselves against the subhuman creatures of this third millennium who prefer ignorance to the knowledge that could generate weapons of mass destruction. Savagery and witchcraft have thus returned. Certain tribes are proud, in fact, to be called Simpletons. Indeed, they have undertaken their own fearful Simplification, a barbaric burning of all books, both sacred and secular. The consequent benightedness is so great that literacy itself has nearly been lost. Some of the novel's most comical scenes occur, in fact, when the monks reverently preserve twentieth century shopping lists. For these survivors of the nuclear holocaust have no way of knowing the import of such phrases as "*Pound pastrami, can kraut, six bagels,*" much less "*Form 1040,*

Uncle Revenue" (27).* The monks solemnly add these trivial tidbits to their Memorabilia, as they call that very small body of recorded knowledge that their Order seeks faithfully to build up.

What are we to make of these strange culture-preservers who belong to the Order of the Blessed Leibowitz? Their work is apocalyptic, as I have suggested, in the original sense of the word. They unveil and bring to light what is otherwise hidden—not only the causes of our culture's deep self-destructiveness but also its potential cure. Because these monastic stockpilers of knowledge love God first and last, and because they are assured that God's kingdom is coming sooner or later, they are also devoted to re-establishing the humanistic and scientific culture that has been virtually lost. They believe that God refuses to be God without the flourishing of human life no less than natural creation, and that the preservation of human lore is a testimony of true faith no less than a sign of true hope and an act of true charity.

I

Fiat Homo, the novel's first section, is perhaps the most powerful. It concerns the plight of Brother Francis Gerard of Utah, a young postulant undergoing his years-long ordeal before finally being ordained as a monk in the Order of the Blessed Leibowitz. His long vigils in the desert—where buzzards hover by day, wolves prowl by night, and brigands threaten always—are atmospherically redolent of our culture of ashes and death. Miller thus enables his readers to experience a world that has been blasted into both physical barrenness and spiritual desolation. Brother Francis' trials also evoke the harsh life of the desert monks of fourth-century Egypt and Syria, even as they suggest the new exactions that our own Dark Age may require. This young monk is made to suffer for his vocation. He wants to devote himself to the life of worship and study, but he discovers that such a life can be had only at the price of extraordinary self-denial. His solitary Lenten fasts from both eating and speaking are exceedingly hard for Francis to keep. Yet the preservation of true faith and learning, Miller suggests, may well require such radical asceticism.

Francis is an imperfect and somewhat comical monk. His desert hunger becomes so writhing that, in a moment of weakness, he eats a

---

*All quotations from Miller are from *A Canticle for Leibowitz* (New York: Bantam-Spectra, 1997) and are documented by page number within the text.

lizard. He also violates his vow of silence by speaking to an anonymous pilgrim wandering amidst the desert loneliness. Either accidentally or providentially, this pilgrim enables Brother Francis to uncover a heretofore hidden fallout shelter containing the final effects of the monastery's patron, Leibowitz himself. When Brother Francis reports this "miraculous" news to his prior and abbot, they take it to be the sheerest delusion, a mark of the noonday madness to which wilderness monastics are prone. The abbot thus punishes the poor postulant for having indulged, as the superior believes, his "execrable vanity" in imagining the whole event.

The future monk has arrived, in fact, at a profound understanding of truth for having been required to reckon hard about the nature of knowledge. Asked to make sure beyond all doubt that he actually encountered the pilgrim rather than hallucinating the whole thing, Brother Francis denies the very premise of the question:

> In his own mind, there was no neat line separating the Natural from the Supernatural order, but rather, an intermediate twilight zone. There were things that were *clearly* natural and there were Things that were *clearly* supernatural, but between these extremes was a region of confusion (his own)—the preternatural[3]—where things made of mere earth, air, fire or water tended to behave disturbingly like *Things*. For Brother Francis, this region included whatever he could see but not understand. (51–52)

The naive novice has rejected, in his own unwitting way, the old scholastic notion of nature and grace. In the pre-Vatican II way of reckoning, supernatural grace is lowered down from above by way of miraculous irruptions into the natural order. In place of such a layer-cake theology that made nature the world's substructure and grace its superstructure, Brother Francis discerns that the two realms are mysteriously enmeshed. The visible and invisible worlds are woven into a seamless web of interlocking realities—divine and human, natural and supernatural. To understand the way the world works requires a radical sense of mystery that only faith can prompt, enabling reason to discern that uncertainty is built into the nature of things and thus indispensable to true knowledge.

The monks' chastened and deepened conception of truth gives them the very widest regard for knowledge. They want to preserve all lore, no matter how obscure or irrelevant. Yet they lack the conceptual framework that would fit their flotsam facts into a coherent whole. Even so, unlike our age, they believe in the Christ in whom all things cohere (Col 1:17), and so they have reason for preserving their jetsam data—that they may eventually redound to the glory of God and the betterment of the human condition.

> It mattered not at all to them that the knowledge they saved was use-less, that much of it was not really knowledge now, was as inscrutable to the monks in some instances as it would be to a wild illiterate boy from the hills; this knowledge was empty of content, its subject mat-ter long since gone. Still, such knowledge had a symbolic structure that was peculiar to itself, and at least the symbol-play could be observed. To observe the way a knowledge-system is knit together is to learn at least a minimum knowledge-of-knowledge, until some-day—someday, or some century—an Integrator would come and all things would be fitted together again. So time mattered [to the monks] not at all. (66)

The monks are not panicked by the long wait for such an Integrator to come. Much of the novel's force derives, in fact, from its evocative sense of time's immensity. We are made to see that cultures rise and fall like the ocean waves, in a vast and seemingly endless succession. The vultures that hover, awaiting their human carrion, are signs that nature finally devours history. Yet the devotees of the Blessed Leibowitz are not deterred in their efforts to preserve culture. They have an enormous patience, because they live not only *within* time but also *beyond* time. They live in the eschatological confidence that the God who in Jesus Christ has indwelt time will also take all of time to work his purposes out. It also teaches them that, while a cultural inheritance can be oblit-erated almost overnight, it takes centuries to build one up.

Brother Francis dies without witnessing any such revival of learning. He does not enjoy even the fruits of his long (and finally successful) effort to have the Blessed Leibowitz canonized as a saint. Returning to Utah from the New Rome with the pope's blessing, he is killed by can-nibals. Yet Miller makes Francis's death seem a negligible loss. It is what the monk has expected, indeed lived for: to die while making his wit-ness in tribute not only to the Christ who has come but also to the Christ who is coming. Francis is, in fact, one of the Order's many mar-tyrs. What finally matters is not the success of their mission but their fidelity to the divine Lightning which has been earthed in the birth, the teaching, the cross, the resurrection, the ascension, and the return of

Jesus Christ. These monks validate their Christian convictions—as realities that cannot be dismissed but that demand our utmost consideration—by the quality of their eschatological deaths no less than the quality of their eschatological lives.

II

The blood of the martyrs proves to be the seed of new life not only for a dead church but also for a dead science, as part 2 makes clear. One of the items that Francis and his fellow monks have preserved is Leibowitz's own blueprint for an electric generator. After the plans had lain dormant for more than a millennium, a monk named Kornhoer has succeeded in reconstructing the light-making machine. In order that its electricity might be used to maximum effect, the solitary lamp is suspended where a crucifix has hung for centuries. The technophobic Brother Armbruster regards such sacrilege as a new scourging of Christ. "Why don't you just hang the witch-light around [Jesus'] neck?" he exclaims (152). The abbot explains that the monastery is not a church, and that the placement of images remains optional. Albeit with a knot in his stomach, the abbot silently asks the crucified Christ whether *he* objects to this temporary relocation of his image. Though the Crucified offers no response, it seems evident that his silence is damning, like that of Christ before Pilate. Electrical light is an obvious improvement over candles, but the monks are in danger of making their invention into an idol—a replacement for Christ.

Soon, alas, the problem of scientific idolatry is made real. In the new southwestern city-state of Texarkana, which is ruled by an illiterate dictator named Hannegan, the young researcher Taddeo Pfardentrott has recovered the rudiments of basic science through the work of his research group called a collegium. Having heard of the monks' Memorabilia, Taddeo and his team of scientists want to inspect the sacred lore. This request puts the Order of Leibowitz in a dilemma. If they decline, they can be accused of hoarding knowledge and thus of preventing a potential integrator from fitting these shards of learning back into their original wholeness. Yet if the pagan scientists are granted access to the Memorabilia, they may develop its science for destructive rather than redemptive purposes.

The monks are right to be suspicious. Taddeo—like many academics—is imbued with an excessive self-regard, having given himself the honorific title of "Thon," perhaps meaning "The Honorable." Taddeo's pride makes him scornful of the past, moreover, as if *he* were himself the creator of physics rather than its humble "rediscoverer" (235), building upon the achievements and mistakes of other scientists. Most alarming of all is Taddeo's cold contempt for the mutant creatures who inhabit the barbaric kingdom of Texarkana. He cannot believe that these pathetic, malformed specimens are the progeny of a once mighty European-American culture. "How can a great and wise civilization have destroyed itself so completely?" he asks. "Perhaps," answers the abbot, "by being materially great and materially wise, and nothing else" (129).

The monks know that to acquire a more than merely material kind of wisdom and greatness requires a drastically new vision. Yet they also know that, while they can provide the religious motive to build a better world, they cannot control those who seek to construct it. Despite several warnings against the naïve and perhaps fatal scientific idolatry of Taddeo and his colleagues, the monks finally grant access to their Memorabilia. The monks believe that it is better to risk the misuse of knowledge than to suppress inquiry. As the Abbot Paulo explains to Taddeo: "We've been waiting a long time to see the world start taking an interest in itself again" (199). Thus does the novel make a wry irony increasingly evident: Abbot Paulo's Christianity is ever so much larger than Thon Taddeo's science. A faith built on the Alpha and Omega of all things, far from fearing science, necessarily encompasses it. Only a theological vision can summon and direct secular learning to its proper ethical ends.

In one of the novel's most important exchanges, Thon Taddeo insists that the work of his scientific collegium exists only at the sufferance of the illiterate autocrat and ruthless politician named Hannegan. Abbot Paulo will not accede to such political expediency. He thus confronts Taddeo with a direct theological decision:

> "[Y]ou promise to begin restoring Man's control over Nature. But who will govern the use of the power to control natural forces? Who will use it? To what end? How will you hold [Hannegan] in check? . . . Mankind will profit, you say. By whose sufferance? The sufferance of a prince who signs his letters X? Or do you really believe that your collegium can stay aloof from his ambitions when he begins to find out that you are valuable to him? . . .
>
> "To serve God first, or to serve Hannegan first—that's your choice."

"I have little choice, then," answered the thon. "Would you have me work for the Church?" The scorn in his voice was unmistakable. (224–25)

The case that Paulo seems to lose by verbal argument he wins by the moral example set by Christians. When Taddeo learns that the papal nuncio to Texarkana has been martyred and his secretary tortured to death for defying Hannegan, the scientist reconsiders his own future as a researcher. He sees that his barbarian boss would be just as willing to eliminate scientists as churchmen. Taddeo seems also to discern that the papal nuncio and his secretary did not die for the sake of their own faith alone, but also for the freedom of others, including a secular scientist such as himself. Taddeo grudgingly accepts the monastic sanctuary offered by the abbot. The novel holds out no sentimental prospect of the scientist's eventual conversion, but it does show him gaining a deep respect for the monks whom he thought to be his enemies. Their preservation of ancient lore, together with the scientist's use of it, has enabled a minimal recovery of civilization. In faithfulness to the gospel's command to love God and neighbor without stint, they have also provided the means for the world to recover its own cultural life. Thus do Christians live toward the *End* by making common cause with those who are not Christians.

III

The novel's final section raises the deeply troubling question of whether it was a good thing for learning thus to be restored. No sooner has social and political order been re-established than the world cannibalizes itself in another nuclear war. In one of the novel's darkest meditations, the new abbot of the Order, whose name is Zerchi, asks whether the human species is "congenitally insane"—whether, lemming like, it is determined to devour itself again every time it recovers its life. Standing before a statue of the martyred Leibowitz, Zerchi ponders this latest holocaust with its billions of corpses. Rather than cast convenient blame, he confesses his horror that the sins of the fathers are indeed repeated unto the fourth and fortieth generation:

> [Abbot Zerchi] fingered the mound of faggots where the wooden martyr stood. *That's where all of us are standing now*, he thought. On the fat kindling of past sins. And some of them are mine. Mine, Adam's,

Herod's, Judas's, Hannegan's, mine. Everybody's. Always culminates in the colossus of the State, somehow, drawing about itself the mantle of godhood, being struck down by the wrath of Heaven. Why? We [monks] shouted it loudly enough—God's to be obeyed by nations as by men. Caesar's to be God's policeman, not His plenipotentiary successor, nor His heir. (282)

This confession of universal sin provides Zerchi and his monks no excuse for a defeatist resignation. They reject the argument that—because religious and moral ideals are impossible to realize, since idolatry is endemic to the human condition—the state must always turn itself into a golden calf that God must pulverize. Christians never despair of their witness to cultures any less than persons. The monks of the sainted Leibowitz know that, with this final wastage of the world, they are faced with a drastic new quandary that requires direct action. The question is no longer what books and manuscripts might be saved but what human lives might be saved.

The imperative first issued by Abbot Paulo to Thon Taddeo—to serve the God of life or the Moloch of death—has now become acute. The local authorities have begun to administer euthanasia to the hopeless victims of the radiation poisoning that resulted from the recent nuclear war. Rather than letting these doomed souls die slow and horrible deaths, Doctor Cors and his Green Star brigade offer to put them out of their pain. They create a so-called Mercy Camp where the dying sufferers can come to be quietly exterminated. Such "mercy-killing" puts Zerchi and his monks to the ultimate test, both morally and spiritually. Should they cooperate in this humanist effort to relieve unendurable agony, or should they declare—unfeeling and merciless as it seems—that there is another mercy that must be preserved at all costs, even bodily anguish?

They find their answer, at least negatively, in the huge statue that stands before the camp gate. It is meant to represent the good-natured human ideal that justifies the extermination of incurable suffering. This composite image has been fashioned from photographs of anonymous faces selected because they *resembled* the perfect parent or the person one would most like to meet, or else because they *contradicted* the appearance of average criminals or individuals one would most want to avoid. The result is a bland, tranquil, androgynous, empty-faced figure. The single word inscribed beneath it is COMFORT. The word has been given its late-modern meaning: to soothe and console in grief or trouble. Neither the statue nor the motto can be reconciled with the image and the gospel to which the monks have offered their lives: the mercy figured in the abbey crucifix. This crucifix gives "comfort" in the original etymological sense: *com-fortis*—to strengthen, to encourage, to support, to invigorate. It inspires the monks to make vehement protest against the false solace that brings death rather than life. They erect their own signs at the death camp: "ABANDON EVERY HOPE YE WHO ENTER HERE" (314).

That the monks employ Dante's inscription over the gates of Hell makes evident the novel's final predicament. At what religious price is human suffering to be ended? Having begun with absolute pity, Doctor Cors and his deadly bringers of comfort end with absolute terror: with the taking of incurably ill life. A godless humanism results, alas, in a hideous anti-humanism. Suffering and the salvation that comes through patient acceptance of it are replaced with painless consolation. In the name of the man-god Comfort, and in denial of the God-Man Jesus, the anti-Christ arrives. The novel thus approaches the terror of the Apocalypse recorded in Revelation.

Yet Walter Miller gives the monks no easy victory over these latter-day mercy killers. In a crucial episode, Father Zerchi urges a mother not to euthanize her badly wounded daughter but to offer the suffering child to Heaven. He assures her that souls who faithfully endure despite their bodily affliction have thus routed Satan and pleased God. The mother replies icily that her child has no capacity to comprehend such theological arguments, only the capacity to feel unendurable pain. "She can hurt," says the mother, "but she can't understand" (316). Zerchi has no ready theodicy to apply to such a mouth-stopping confession. Neither can he silence the argument of Doctor Cors, who engages him in one of the novel's most telling exchanges:

> "Listen, Father. They sit there and they look at you. Some scream. Some cry. Some just sit there. All of them say, 'Doctor, what can I do?' And what am I supposed to answer? Say nothing? Say, 'You can die, that's all.' What would you say?"
> "Pray."
> "Yes, you would, wouldn't you? Listen, pain is the only evil I know about. It's the only one I can fight."
> "Then God help you."
> "Antibiotics help me more." (298–99)

Like the Jesus who remained silent before Pilate, Zerchi does not reply. He knows that Doctor Cors cannot understand that, though antibiotics are surely indispensable, they cannot heal the real human hurt: the macerated soul and conscience. The angry Zerchi turns away from the opaque Cors to his fellow monks. He asks them how civilization could have allowed itself to accept Doctor Cors' two clearly heretical claims—that society alone determines whether an act is right or wrong, and that pain is the only evil. For a Christian like Zerchi, the real problem is not theodicy—how to justify the goodness of God in the face of overwhelming suffering, especially the uncomprehending suffering of children. The real problem is how to direct human life to ends that are redemptive rather than expedient, ends that are not humanly devised and managed, but ends that enable people to live for a higher good than the avoidance of pain, even agonizing pain. Such a life entails suffering—suffering far more moral and spiritual than bodily and physical.

Here is the point at which the novel becomes most eschatologically relevant to our own time. Absent any belief in the God who himself has died for the world's pain, Zerchi confesses, men and women seek to avoid anguish at all costs—indeed, to create a pain-free planet. Unable to manufacture such a comfortable world, our species turns bitter and destructive. The resulting carnage—whether in personal fury or political holocaust—is theological at its core. The dying and hallucinating Zerchi reveals its nature in his final confession to the euthanizing Cors:

> "Really, Doctor Cors, the evil to which you even you should have referred was not suffering, but the unreasoning fear of suffering. *Metus doloris.* Take it together with its positive equivalent, the craving for worldly security, for Eden, and you might have your "root of evil," Doctor Cors. To minimize suffering and to maximize security were natural and proper ends of society and Caesar. But then they became the only ends, somehow, the only basis of law—a perversion. Inevitably, then, in seeking only them, we found only their opposites: maximum suffering and minimum security. . . .
>
> "Listen, my dear Cors, why don't you forgive God for allowing pain. If He didn't allow it, human courage, bravery, nobility, and sacrifice would all be meaningless things. . . .
>
> "Maybe that's what we forgot to mention. . . . Bombs and tantrums, when the world grew bitter because the world somehow fell short of a half-remembered Eden. The bitterness was essentially against God." (330, 332).

Here lies one of the novel's most searing insights—that the world consumes itself in violence springing from an unconfessed fury against God for having created a suffering-laden world. The ultimate means of revenge against God for having fashioned a pain-filled planet is to uncreate his creation, to destroy it.

Miller shows the church refusing such a refusal in the most drastic of ways. The new Pope Gregory has ceased to pray for the peace of the world. Instead, he offers a Mass against the Heathen and another Mass in Time of War. There comes a pass, Miller suggests, when the church can no longer cast its hope with a self-cannibalizing culture but must indeed damn and anathematize it. Though the pope himself retires to the mountains to meditate, to pray for justice, and presumably to die with the world's own extinction, he has ordered the Leibowitzian monks to insure that the Hope of All Worlds does not die. In obedience to the papal command, they violate state regulations by sending a missile to Alpha Centauri, the nearest star cluster, where a small human colony has been established. They fill the spacecraft with bishops, priests, and monks. The authorities at New Rome know that this decision will cause great scandal, as indeed it has scandalized many readers. That ordinary survivors of the nuclear bonfire were not first rescued seems extremely self-serving. "Let the church survive even if others be lost," Miller seems to be saying. Yet the monks are convinced that it will do humanity no true good merely to survive if the gospel itself is lost. This is the single memory, the single hope, the one canticle that can stanch the bitterness against God that causes humanity to incinerate itself. Among all the world's narratives, this is the sole Story of the God who allowed himself to be extinguished that the world's light might burn with life rather than death. The suffering that God requires of his creation, Miller's novel starkly affirms, is the suffering that God himself has supremely endured.

That human life finds its true destiny in suffering mutually born by God and humanity is figured in the strange bicephalous woman named Mrs. Grales. An illiterate vendor of tomatoes, this creature with two heads is the frightful victim of a genetic mutation that was caused, it seems, by fallout from earlier atomic wars. The resulting deformity gives her a blank second head whom she has named Rachel. If ever there were cause for bitterness against God, surely the grotesque Mrs. Grales has it. Yet in one of the novel's most remarkable scenes, she requests Father Zerchi to grant forgiveness to God for making her the hideous creature that she is. "Mayn't an old tumater woman," she asks, "forgive

Him just a little for His Justice? Afor I be asking His shriv'ness on me?" (325). The answer, though implied, is an unambiguous yes. Radical faith requires a radical acceptance, a submission to the will of God so drastic that it amounts to the forgiveness of God for creating a world so free that it can go wretchedly wrong. Not to have pity *on* God, as with Doctor Cors, is to seek terrible human substitutes for the pity *of* God.

The novel ends as the blinding light of the final holocaust begins to incinerate the world, and as the failing Mrs. Grales receives her final absolution from Father Zerchi. When the old woman dies, the heretofore lifeless head of Rachel gradually comes to consciousness and speech. The startled Father Zerchi—knowing that the end is near—attempts to baptize the newborn woman, but she refuses. And when he offers her the eucharist, she again rejects it. Why? Who is this exceedingly odd character named Rachel? As a creature neither conceived in sin nor having had any occasion for sin, she possesses a "primal innocence" (336) that surely evokes the Virgin Mary in its quality. She seems to be a figure of the remnant church that God raises up even when the world destroys itself. This Rachel is a dispenser rather than a receiver of grace, as she places the consecrated body of Christ in the dying abbot's hand. No longer weeping for her lost children like the Rachel of both Jeremiah's and Matthew's prophecies, this new Rachel embodies the hope that can save the world because it is the hope that dissolves all bitterness and thus brings forth life rather than death. It comes whenever the saving words are pronounced: whether by the Virgin Mary at the Annunciation, by Christ himself in Gethsemane, or by the young monk who will lead the expedition to Alpha Centauri—*Fiat voluntas tua*: Thy will be done. These are the truly eschatological words. They unveil and thus disclose that evil consists, at its core, in the refusal to make this deepest of all utterances. Yet they also reveal that to say and sing them is to live for the End that is the one true and eternal Beginning called Paradise.

NOTES

Chapter 1: The Scandalous Baptism of Harry Ashfield in Flannery O'Connor's "The River"

1. *The Habit of Being: Letters of Flannery O'Connor*, selected and edited by Sally Fitzgerald (New York: Farrar Straus Giroux, 1979), 360.

Chapter 2: The Quest for Christian Vocation in Walker Percy's *The Moviegoer*

1. Barth, Karl, and Geoffrey William Bromiley. *The Doctrine of the Word of God: Prolegomena to Church Dogmatics* vol 4. (Edinburgh: T. & T. Clark, 1975), 519.

Chapter 4: The Witness Made by Martyrdom in T. S. Eliot's *Murder in the Cathedral*

1. Robert Bolt, *A Man for All Seasons* (New York: Vintage, 1962), 81.

2. G. K. Chesterton, *A Short History of England* (London: Chatto and Windus, 1938), 77–78.

3. T. S. Eliot, *Four Quartets* (Harcourt Brace Jovanovich, 1971), 30.

4. *The Four Quartets*, 57.

Chapter 5: Hospitality as the Gift Greater than Tolerance in G. K. Chesterton's *The Ball and the Cross*

1. Originally delivered as a lecture at *The Dialogue of Cultures*: A Conference Sponsored by the University of Notre Dame Center for Ethics and Culture, December 1, 2007.

2. G. K. Chesterton, *The Collected Works of G. K. Chesterton*, Volume XXVIII: *The Illustrated London News, 1908-1910*, ed. Lawrence J. Clipper (San Francisco: Ignatius, 1987), 194.

3. G. K. Chesterton, *The Everlasting Man* (Garden City, NY: Image, 1955, originally published 1925), 184–85.

4. G. K. Chesterton, *Charles Dickens* (New York: Schocken, 1965, originally published 1906), 10.

5. This is not to deny that he had scorching things to say about such modern notions "as that law is above right, or right outside reason, or things are only as we think them, or everything is relative to a reality that is not there." *Heretics* (London: Bodley Head, 1960; first published in 1905), 146.

6. Quoted in Kristen Deede Johnson, *Theology, Political Theory, and Pluralism* (New York: Cambridge, 2007), 15.

7. It has been wisely observed that we ought to lament the failure of liberalism all the more plaintively, since it constitutes the noblest and best attempt to deal with the modern pluralist predicament.

8. All quotations from "A Letter Concerning Toleration" are taken from William Popple's 1689 translation of Locke's Latin original, *Epistola de Tolerantia*. (http://www.constitution.org/jl/tolerati.htm) Voltaire translated it into French five years later, though not without showing his witty contempt for religion: "[England] is the country of sects. An Englishman, as a freeman, goes to Heaven by whatever road he pleases."

9. Jefferson agreed. "The legitimate powers of government," he would add a century later, "extend to such acts only as are injurious to others. But it does me no injury for my neighbor to say that there are twenty Gods, or no God. It neither picks my pocket nor breaks my leg." Thomas Jefferson, "Notes on Virginia" [1782] (http://etext.virginia.edu/jefferson/quotations/)

10. Locke's notion of natural law has but faint resemblance to its medieval predecessors. Hence Lord Herbert of Cherbury's rather thin Lockean formulation of the five reasonable propositions that, according to him, all people of all times have held, without regard to race or religion, except when obscured by the distortions and accretions of so-called revealed truth: (1) that God exists; (2) that he ought to be worshipped; (3) that virtue and piety are the chief part of worship; (4) that there must be repentance for crimes and vices; (5) that there are rewards and punishments in the life to come based on the ways we have acquitted ourselves in this earthly life.

11. Locke denies even this authority to the churches, regarding them as purely voluntary organizations whose sovereignty resides solely in their members, not in their ministers or deacons, their presbyters or vestry, much less in their bishops and prelates who represent the authority of Christ himself.

12. William T. Cavanaugh, "The City: Beyond Secular Parodies," in *Radical Orthodoxy*, ed. John Milbank, Catherine Pickstock, and Graham Ward (New York: Routledge, 1999), 191, 189, 190, 192. The rise of the modern nation-state is premised on the elevation of this isolated and autonomous individual who is defined largely by his accumulation of privately owned goods. As essentially propertied creatures, individuals have relation to each other largely by means of self-protecting contracts. These contracts have a temporal duration, moreover, even as they are contingent upon the agreement of the contracting parties. Contracts can also be dissolved by limiting clauses or by mutual consent. No longer is there an unbreakable bond that unites the entire body politic in devotion to common ends. The basis of such politics has indeed disappeared— namely, the indissoluble covenant between God and his people, as this bond is sealed through the sacraments. "It is not surprising," declares Cavanaugh, "that . . . Descartes placed 'among the [antique] excesses all of the promises by which one curtails something of one's freedom,' that Milton wrote a treatise on divorce, or that Kant condemned the covenants that bind one's descendants" (190).

13. In *Planned Parenthood v. Casey*, the 1992 Supreme Court case upholding *Roe v. Wade*, the justices (Anthony Kennedy is rumored to be the actual author) confirmed this Enlightenment assumption by declaring that all Americans have the privilege of construing reality for themselves: "At the heart of liberty is the right to define one's own concept of existence, of meaning, of the universe, and of the mystery of life" (http://www.law.cornell.edu/supct/html/91-744.ZO.html).

Consider, by contrast, Abraham Lincoln's sharp riposte to Stephen Douglas's insistence that Southerners should have the right to choose slavery if they so wished and so voted: "No one has the right to choose to do what is so fundamentally wrong." Qtd. in Wilson D. Miscamble, C.S.C., *Keeping the Faith, Making a Difference* (Notre Dame, IN: Ave Maria, 2000), 100.

14. This argument is made most convincingly by Michael Sandel in *Democracy's Discontents: America in Search of a Public Philosophy* (Cambridge, MA: Harvard, 1996).

15. Wendy Brown, *Regulating Aversion: Tolerance in the Age of Identity and Empire* (Princeton: Princeton University Press, 2006), 32.

16. Alasdair MacIntyre argues that, precisely because the contemporary state cannot be "evaluatively neutral . . . it cannot be generally trusted to promote any worthwhile set of values, including those of autonomy and liberty." "Toleration and the goods of conflict," in *The Tasks of Philosophy: Selected Essays on Ethics and Politics*, vol. 2 (New York: Cambridge University Press, 2006), 213–14.

17. Jeff Polet, who teaches political science at Hope College, reminds me that keen political prudence must be exercised in the practice of hospitality, since it is also our Christian duty to protect the innocent. To a rapist breaking into our daughter's bedroom, we would not offer hospitality. I suspect that the church itself must remain both the locus of such prudential judgments and also the place where aliens and enemies are welcomed.

18. Among the studies of hospitality that I have found most helpful, I have relied most fully on the work of my former student, Elizabeth Newman, *Untamed Hospitality: Welcoming God and Other Strangers* (Grand Rapids, MI: Brazos, 2007). The work of Mennonite peacemakers in contemporary Iraq and Palestine and Israel are examples of such Christian hospitality. They live in the midst of Muslim and Jewish groups that are hostile not only to each other but also to Christians, offering them both shelter and friendship, thus demonstrating "a more excellent way" (1 Cor 12:31).

19. Lest anyone fear that Chesterton is engaged in anything other than metaphor and trope: "That the duel kills seems to me a comparatively trifling matter; football and fox-hunting and the London hospitals frequently do that. The only rational objection to the duel is that it invokes a most painful and sanguinary proceeding in order to settle a question, and does not settle it." "The Patriotic Idea," *Chesterton Review* 30, 3 & 4 (Fall/Winter 2004): 229.

20. Alison Milbank, *Chesterton and Tolkien as Theologians* (London: T&T Clark, 2007), 33.

21. Chesterton thus makes the surprising claim that, while "black and catastrophic" pain attracts the immature artist, "joy is a far more elusive and elvish matter, since it is our reason for existing, and a very feminine reason; it mingles with every breath we draw and every cup of tea we drink." Precisely because joy remains largely unrecognized in its invisible ubiquity, it requires an extraordinary mode of expression. "And of all the varied forms of the literature of joy," Chesterton concludes, "the form most truly worthy of moral reverence and artistic ambition is the form called 'farce'—or its wilder shape in pantomime." "A Defence of Farce," in *The Defendant* (London: J. M. Dent and Sons, 1940), 124–25.

22. "Never has there been so little discussion about the nature of men as now, when, for the first time, anyone can discuss it. The old [authoritarian] restriction meant that only the orthodox were allowed to discuss religion. Modern liberty means that nobody is allowed to discuss it. Good taste, the last and vilest of human superstitions, has succeeded in silencing us where all the rest have failed." G. K. Chesterton, "Introduction" to *Heretics* (London: Bodley Head, 1960; originally published in 1905), 7.

23. Dogmas are such mind-and-soul nourishing solids. "Man may be defined as an animal that makes dogmas. As he piles doctrine on doctrine and conclusion on conclusion in the formation of some tremendous scheme of philosophy and religion, he is, in the only legitimate sense of which the expression is capable, becoming more and more human. When he drops one doctrine after another in a refined skepticism, when he declines to tie himself to a system, when he says that he has outgrown definitions, when he says that he disbelieves in finality, when, in his own imagination, he sits as God, holding no form of creed but contemplating them all, then he is by that very process sinking slowly backward into the vagueness of the vagrant animals and the unconsciousness of the grass. Trees have no dogmas. Turnips are singularly broad-minded." *Heretics*, 288–89.

24. Chesterton was early to discern that tolerance becomes impossible when belief no longer prevails, for then there is no transcendent Order that makes such tolerance possible: "A nation with a root religion will be tolerant. A nation with no religion will be bigoted" (G. K. Chesterton, "The Sectarian Society," in *A Miscellany of Men* (Philadelphia: Dufour, 1969; originally published in 1912), 78.

25. It is noteworthy that Turnbull and MacIan's contest is based on mutual truth-telling, and thus on the common assumption of at least a minimal doctrine of natural law. Neither hospitality nor friendship is possible when this most basic fundament of human existence is denied.

26. Whether directly or indirectly, MacIan has learned from Saint Augustine that God is the root and aim, the source and end, of all true being. Without God, there is literally non-being: nothing.

27. I have gratefully learned from Alasdair MacIntyre that this term is more apt than *materialism*, since Christians have an intransigent regard for material reality as inherently good; indeed, as that which the soul shapes into form. The Incarnation made the redemption of pagan materialism (perhaps as figured in Lucretius) virtually inevitable, says Chesterton:

> "There really was a new reason for regarding the senses, and the sensations of the body, . . . with a reverence at which great Aristotle would have stared, and no man in the ancient world could have begun to understand. . . . It was no longer possible for the soul to despise the senses, which had been the organs of something that was more than man. Plato might despise the flesh; but God had not despised it. The senses had truly become sanctified; as they are blessed one by one at a Catholic baptism. . . . When once Christ had risen, it was inevitable that Aristotle should rise again." *Saint Thomas Aquinas: The Dumb Ox* (NY: Doubleday, 1956), 118–19

28. MacIan more fully and funnily articulates the character of his Thomistic faith in this declaration to Turnbull: "I was born and bred and taught in a complete universe. The supernatural was not natural, but it was perfectly reasonable. Nay, the supernatural is to me more reasonable than the natural: for the supernatural is a direct message [i.e., revelation] from God, who is reason. I was taught that some things are natural and some things divine. I mean that some things are mechanical and some things are divine. But there is the great difficulty, Turnbull. The great difficulty is that, according to my teaching, you are divine" (58).

29. Chesterton, *Saint Thomas Aquinas*, 158–59. Chesterton is alluding, of course, to the then-recent discoveries of Einstein.

30. This is the salutary truth that MacIan has learned from Turnbull—that the cosmos does not readily conform to the traditional and hierarchical ordering once known as the Great Chain of Being, as the word "mechanical" indicates in this confession. Even so, he will not yield in his conviction that Turnbull is not a piece of physicalist machinery but an immortal soul in the making.

31. Nietzsche did indeed extol the dawning age of violence: "We now confront a succession of a few warlike centuries that have no parallel in history; in short, . . . we have entered *the classical age of war*, of scientific and at the same time popular war on the largest scale (in weapons, talents, and discipline). All coming centuries will look back on it with envy and awe for its perfection." *The Gay Science*, trans. Walter Kaufmann (New York: Vintage, 1974), 318.

32. Stephen R. L. Clark, *G. K. Chesterton: Thinking Backward, Looking Forward* (Philadelphia: Templeton Foundation, 2006) 58.

33. While these incarcerated souls have all been provided the food and space necessary for living, they have been deprived of the freedom that makes life worth living. Chesterton thus prophesies the coming dehumanization of modern life, the ostensible freedom that is but disguised slavery:

> "For these great scientific organizers insisted that a man should be healthy even if he was miserable. . . . It seemed never to have occurred to them that the benefit of exercise belongs to the benefit of liberty. They had not entertained the suggestion that the open air is only one of the advantages of the open sky. They administered air in secret, but in sufficient doses, as if it were a medicine. They suggested walking, as if no man had ever felt inclined to walk. Above all, the asylum authorities insisted on their own extraordinary cleanliness" (147).

34. The question of sanity pervades the entirety of Chesterton's work. His treatise on Distributism is entitled *An Outline of Sanity*, and in *Orthodoxy* he argues that the fundamental modern condition is not sinfulness and rebellion against God, but rather madness: either a deranged rationalism or else an equally insane emotivism. Nor was madness a mere theoretical concern, for Chesterton himself was almost reduced to insanity while he was a student at the Slade School of Art. In a chapter of his *Autobiography* (London: Burns Oates & Washburn, 1938) entitled "How To Be a Lunatic," he confesses his near descent into a mental hell: "At this time I did not very clearly distinguish between dreaming and waking; not only as a mood, but as a metaphysical doubt, I felt as if everything might be a dream. It was as if I had projected the universe from within, with all its trees and stars; and that is so near to the notion of being God that it is manifestly even nearer to going mad" (92).

35. The Mental Deficiency Act (not repealed until 1959) established "four classes of 'mental defectives': idiots, imbeciles, the feeble minded, and moral defectives" (Clark, 215n20). The bill was prompted largely by public alarm over "the feebleness of English troops during the Boer War." Adam Schwartz, "G. K. C.'s Methodical Madness: Sanity and Social Control in Chesterton," *Renascence* 49.1 (Fall, 1996): 31. Schwartz offers the most convincing study of Chesterton's fierce opposition to eugenics, especially as its advocates sought to rid England of those deemed insane. Schwarz shows the remarkable similarity, despite their antithetical viewpoints on other matters, between Chesterton and Michel Foucault.

36. G. K. Chesterton, *Eugenics and Other Evils: An Argument against the Scientifically Organized State*, first published 1922 (Seattle: Inkling Books, 2000). Such foul physicalism has not ceased to exist during the century since *The Ball and the Cross* was first published. Oliver Wendell Holmes, who served as a Justice of the United States Supreme Court from 1902 to 1932, went even further than the Churchill proposal. Unsatisfied with the sterilizing of "imbeciles,"

Holmes advocated the execution of "unfit" infants, eliminating "at once with instant execution what now is left for nature to destroy." "I believe," he added "that the wholesale regeneration [of our culture] which so many now seem to expect, if it can be helped by conscious, coordinated human effort, cannot be affected appreciably by tinkering with the institution of property, but only by taking in hand life and trying to build a race." Qtd. in Albert Alschuler, *Law Without Values: The Life, Work, and Legacy of Justice Holmes* (University of Chicago, 2000), 27. In his desire to rid the world of the "unworthy," Holmes was joined by many other notable figures, including (among others) Margaret Sanger, H. G. Wells, Beatrice and Sidney Webb, G. B. Shaw, Virginia Woolf, Clarence Darrow, Harold Laski, and Calvin Coolidge. "America must be kept American," Coolidge wrote in 1921. "Biological laws show that Nordics deteriorate when mixed with other races." Qtd. in Barry Bruinius, *Better for All the World: The Secret History of Forced Sterilization and America's Quest for Racial Purity* (New York: Knopf, 2006), 266.

37. Quoted by James Glanz in "Physicist Ponders God, Truth and 'a Final Theory,'" *New York Times*, January 25, 2000.

38. MacIan explains that an "apocalypse is the opposite of a dream. A dream is falser than the outer life. But the end of the world is more actual than the world it ends" (166). He means, I suspect, that an apocalypse brings the world to its true *telos*, the finality and completion toward which it has been aiming from the outset. Lacking any such *finis*, dreams falsify the real world by making it either better or worse than it is.

39. That Turnbull is no mere physicalist has been indicated earlier in the novel when he is caught in a terrible inconsistency after ridiculing the Mass that his future bride makes the center of her life:

> "You think it only a bit of bread," said the girl, and her lips tightened ever so little.
>
> "I know it is only a bit of bread," said Turnbull, with violence.
>
> She flung back her open face and smiled. "Then why did you refuse to eat it?"
>
> James Turnbull made a little step backward, and for the first time in his life there seemed to break out and blaze in his head thoughts that were not his own. (100)

40. The novel's only complementarity may be found in the marriages that our adversaries are about to make: MacIan to a non-Christian and Turnbull to a Catholic. Yet there is little suggestion that opposites are necessary to each other even here. The Catholic MacIan cannot marry an unbeliever with the church's blessings, and so she will presumably become Catholic before their wedding. And since Turnbull is converted in the end, he and his new bride will share their Christianity as their deepest source of their mutuality.

41. *Orthodoxy* (San Francisco: Ignatius, 1995; originally published in 1905), 32–33.

"It is amusing to notice that many of the moderns, whether skeptics or mystics, have taken as their sign a certain eastern symbol, which is the very symbol of . . . ultimate nullity. When they wish to represent eternity, they represent it by a serpent with his tail in his mouth. . . . For the circle is perfect and infinite in its nature; but it is fixed for ever in its size; it can never be larger or smaller. But the cross, though it has at its heart a collision and a contradiction, can extend its four arms for ever without altering its shape. Because it has a paradox in its centre it can grow without changing. The circle returns upon itself and is bound. The cross opens its arms to the four winds; it is a signpost for free travellers."

42. The church is not always the adulterous and whoring bride of Christ. She also has her moments of purity, especially when refusing to resort to the violence of the nations: "The State, in all lands and ages, has created a machinery of punishment, more bloody and brutal in some places than others, but bloody and brutal everywhere. The Church is the only institution that ever attempted to create a machinery of pardon. The Church is the only thing that ever attempted by system to pursue and discover crimes, not in order to avenge, but in order to forgive them. The stake and rack were merely the weaknesses of religion; its snobberies, its surrenders to the world. Its speciality—or, if you like, its oddity—was this merciless mercy; the unrelenting sleuthhound who seeks to save and not to slay." G. K. Chesterton, "The Divine Detective," in *A Miscellany of Men* (Philadelphia: Dufour, 1969; first published 1912), 155–56.

43. The coronation ceremony specifies "the Delivery of the Orb" to the new monarch as follows (http://www.oremus.org/liturgy/coronation/cor1953b.html):

> Then shall the Orb with the Cross be brought from the Altar by the Dean of Westminster and delivered into the Queen's right hand by the Archbishop, saying:
>> Receive this Orb set under the Cross,
>> and remember that the whole world
>> is subject to the Power and Empire
>> of Christ our Redeemer.
> Then shall the Queen deliver the Orb to the Dean of Westminster, to be by him laid upon the Altar.

44. I am grateful to several friends who have helped, whether directly or indirectly, with this essay, especially Matt Waller, Bob Ratcliff, Jeff Polet,

Stanley Hauerwas, Adam Schwartz, Barry Harvey, Elizabeth Newman, Scott Moore, and Alasdair MacIntyre.

Chapter 6: Doubt about the Goodness of God in C. S. Lewis's *Till We Have Faces*

1. C. S. Lewis, *George MacDonald: An Anthology* (New York: MacMillan, 1947), 85.

2. Michel Quenot, *The Icon: Window on the Kingdom* (Crestwood, NY: St. Vladimir's Seminary Press, 1991), 147.

Chapter 7: Christian Living toward the End of Time in Walter Miller's *A Canticle for Leibowitz*

1. Earlier versions of chapter 7 were published as "Lest the World's Amnesia Be Complete: A Reading of Walter Miller's *A Canticle for Leibowitz*" in *Perspectives in Religious Studies* 27, 1 (Spring 2000): 83–97; and in *Religion & Literature* 33, 1 (Spring 2001): 23–41. It is reprinted here with permission granted by *Perspectives in Religious Studies* and by the University of Notre Dame, *Religion & Literature*, Issue 33.1 (Spring 2001).

2. That most of us cannot read the Latin words and phrases with which Miller lards his novel—much less recognize his many allusions to the offices and practices of the Catholic church—reveals the extent to which we have barbarously squandered our own linguistic and religious patrimony. I have offered my own annotations for the novel at http://homepages.baylor.edu/ralph_wood.

3. *The Modern Catholic Dictionary* defines *preternatural gifts* as "favors granted by God above and beyond the powers or capacities of the nature that receives them but not beyond those of all created nature. . . . They include the three great privileges to which human beings have no title—infused knowledge, absence of concupiscence, and bodily immortality. Adam and Eve possessed these gifts before the Fall." John A. Hardon (Garden City, N.Y.: Doubleday, 1980).